The World of
BUSINES

A textbook for GCSE

Martin Smidman

HEINEMANN
EDUCATIONAL

Heinemann Educational,
a division of Heinemann Educational Books Ltd,
Halley Court, Jordan Hill, Oxford OX2 8EJ

OXFORD   LONDON   EDINBURGH   MADRID
ATHENS   BOLOGNA   PARIS   MELBOURNE
SYDNEY   AUCKLAND   SINGAPORE   TOKYO
IBADAN   NAIROBI   HARARE   GABORONE
PORTSMOUTH NH (USA)

First published 1989

92 93 94 95 96 12 11 10 9 8 7 6 5 4 3

British Library Cataloguing in Publication Data
Smidman, Martin
The world of business.
1. Business enterprise
I. Title
338.6
ISBN 0–435–45552–4

Designed, illustrated and typeset by Gecko Ltd,
Bicester, Oxon

Printed and bound in Great Britain by The Bath Press, Avon

Contents

Preface and Acknowledgements

Preface

In common with most subjects, GCSE Business Studies has begun to move away from the classroom and towards the investigation of 'real life' situations. On the other hand, the major part of the final mark is still on an examination that demands a thorough *knowledge* of the subject and also the *skills* to solve problems within it. This textbook aims to equip the full range of GCSE Business Studies students with the means to fulfil all of these aspects of the course. It was written with the closest reference to all the syllabuses and it is hoped that it will also be of considerable assistance to those studying *Business and Information Studies*.

A note from the author

I would like to thank Malcolm Dawson of George Stevenson High School of Killingworth for reading the manuscript and making helpful criticisms and my colleagues Joan Briggs and Marion Craig for using some of the material and giving suggestions, also to my wife Judith who gave me a lot of ideas for illustrations and created the conditions for me to complete the work. Needless to say, I alone am responsible for any errors.

Acknowledgements

The author and publisher would like to thank the following
for permission to reproduce copyright material:

Advertising Standards Authority: Figs 6.9, 6.10
Anna Alston and Ruth Miller, authors of *Equal
Opportunities: A Careers Guide*, published by Penguin
1987 (new edition due in 1990): Fig. 4.8
BBC: Fig. 4.11
Body Shop: Fig. 2.9
The Boots Company PLC: Fig. 2.12
British Airways: Fig. 6.19
The British Petroleum Company PLC: Fig. 6.18
"Loulou" by Parfums Cacharel: Fig. 6.25
Camera Press: (Tom Blau) Fig. 3.1
            (Le Lynx) Fig. 7.8
            (Roger Wood) Fig. 3.7 (1)
J Allan Cash Ltd: Figs 6.15, 6.16, 6.17, 7.1(B), 9.6
Derwent Valley Foods: Figs 6.26, 6.27
Equal Opportunities Commission: Figs 4.9, 4.10
Financial Times: extract on pp. 28 by Anthony Moreton,
published 4 February 1984.
Format Photographers Ltd: (Brenda Prince) Figs 1.4(A),
            4.4, 4.7
            (Jenny Matthews) Fig. 3.7(3)
Sally & Richard Greenhill: Fig. 7.9(B)
The Guardian: Fig. 4.17
Robert Harding Picture Library: Fig. 1.4(B)
HMSO: Figs 1.9, 2.5, 4.6, 7.6, 7.11
HM Treasury: Figs. 7.3, 7.21
IBM UK Ltd: Figs 9.1, 9.3
Lloyd's of London: Fig. 8.4
The Market Research Society: Fig. 6.7
'Archie' Miles: Fig. 8.6
National Business and Information Studies Project,

Curriculum Development Centre, Southampton for the
Tyne and Wear Case Study and Figs 10.4–10.7
Thomas Nelson & Sons for figure from *The British Isles* by
David Waugh (Fig. 1.10)
Mini Enterprise in Schools project-centre for Education
and Industry at the University of Warwick
Network Photographers: (Mike Abrahams) Fig. 7.9
            (Martin Mayer) Fig 3.7(2)
            (John Sturrock) Fig. 4.18
Nissan: Figs 2.4, 2.6
Parker Knoll Furniture Ltd: Fig. 1.1
Popperfoto: Figs 7.21, 8.7
Science Photo Library: Fig. 9.2
Sketchley PLC: Fig. 2.12
W H Smith Ltd: Fig. 2.12
Sock Shop International PLC: Fig. 2.12
Liz Sommerville: Fig. 2.12
Frank Spooner: Figs 4.15, 4.16
STC: Fig. 9.9
Stock Exchange: Fig. 7.14
Suma Wholefoods: Fig. 2.9
Tie Rack: Fig. 2.12
Topham Picture Library: Fig. 7.1(A)
Bob Watkins: Figs 6.25, 9.10, 9.11
Wimpy International: Fig. 2.12
Andrew Wiard: Fig. 4.14

It has not been possible in all cases to trace copyright
holders; the publishers would be glad to hear from any
such unacknowledged copyright holders.

1.1 What is 'business'?

There are two ways of taking part in any activity – one is to work by yourself and do whatever you can; the other is by working with other people. Think about any team ball game – many sides have a 'talented individual', the player who has a lot of skill but just plays for him- or herself. The team may be in a good attacking position with a number of players waiting for the ball and in a good position to shoot. The 'talented individual' may personally try to score from a difficult angle and narrowly miss – when a well-placed pass might have brought about a goal for the team.

What people have found throughout history is that everybody benefits from working together. This is especially true when essentials, such as food or housing, are in short supply. A few people could make a grab for them; they may do all right (although they may cut each other's throats in the rush), but the majority of people will lose out. If, on the other hand, everyone gets together and concentrates on what they are each best at, everyone will benefit. Working together is known as **co-operation** and doing what you are best at is known as **specialisation**.

You may wonder what this has to do with 'business'. Well, imagine that you could not go to the shops to buy your food but had to catch or grow your own; you could not go to an estate agent to buy or rent a house but had to build your own; you could not go to the clothes shop to buy your clothes but had to make your own . . . would you like that? You would certainly have to be a 'Jack of all trades' – but you would be a master of none.

ACTIVITY

Hold a 'brainstorming session' to work out the different types of job or service that you and your parents make use of at different times. Beside each one make a list of the skills and qualities that you think might be needed to do that job. Draw a table of the final result.

In order to avoid such a situation, there are people who do those jobs for us – the farmer, the builder, the tailor. They are **specialists** who spend all their time doing those jobs. Thus they grow more food, build more houses, and make more clothes than they could possibly use themselves. In other words, they create a **surplus** (make a note of its meaning). They swop their surplus in return for money which they use to buy other people's surpluses. After all, farmers need homes and clothes, builders need food and clothes and tailors need food and homes.

So the farmer, the builder and the tailor set up **businesses** to provide those goods for people who need them. They hope to make at least enough money to enable them to buy the other goods they need in order to survive. If they are lucky they will earn a little more. The most important thing is to make goods that people need and are willing to buy. A successful business manages to do that; a failure does not.

Anyone running a business has three basic decisions to make: **what** to produce, **how much** and at what **price**. If you always bear that in mind, what follows will make sense.

Fig. 1.1 A specialist furniture-maker

1.2 What do businesses need?

As we will see during the course businesses have many needs if they are to be successful. At this stage we can limit the question to that of **resources**. Resources are items that are needed to make the product. Think of a typical factory. What does it need?

It needs:

- **land** on which to build the factory;
- **labour** to make the product;
- **capital** – the machinery and all the other 'non-human' items which help the workers to make the product;
- **entrepreneurship** – these are the 'management skills' needed to bring the other factors together and make them work and also the provider of money to buy them.

These things are called **factors of production**.

What different types of business are there?

There are many different types of business, which can be grouped in three broad categories. For instance, think about the *stages* in the making of a table – its **production** – before it actually reaches your home:

1 Chop down the tree.
2 Make the table from the wood.
3 Sell the finished article.

Stage 1 is the finding of the raw material – in this case the wood. This is called **primary production**.

Stage 2 is the actual making of the article and is called **secondary production**.

Stage 3 is the distribution and selling of the finished article. This is called **tertiary production**. Tertiary industry includes businesses that provide a service, such as banking and insurance. Anything that the customer 'directly' uses, such as a shop or a hairdresser, is known as a **direct service**. Aids to business, usually financial, are known as **commerce**.

EXERCISE

Look through the following list of industries and put each into one of the categories of production:

Building	Mining
Motor manufacture	Stock Exchange
Wholesalers	Fishing
Farming	Teaching
Accountancy	

Think up three more industries of each type and put them under the correct heading. Copy Fig. 1.3 and fill it in with the names of the industries on your list.

In pairs, compare your lists to see whether you both agree. Discuss why you may have put one or two industries in a different category. If you have difficulty with placing any, discuss your reasons with your partner or your teacher.

As you can see, one industry **depends** upon another. If the forester did not cut down the tree the furniture maker

Fig. 1.2 The stages of production

would not be able to make the table; if the furniture maker did not make the table the furniture shop would not be able to sell it. So we say that industry is **interdependent**.

EXERCISE

Write a short essay summarising what you have learned in this unit. Make sure that you include the following points:

(a) Why people co-operate in making things and why they specialise.
(b) Why people set up 'in business'.
(c) Why we swop goods for money rather than for other goods.
(d) The factors of production that businesses need to make goods.
(e) What different types of industry there are.
(f) How these different types of industry depend on each other.

Use examples from real life wherever you can and try to include as many as possible of the business terms that you have learned from the unit. Use them in the correct place and show that you understand their meaning. Remember to write it as an essay and *not* just as a collection of answers to the questions.

> ## EXTENSION ACTIVITY
> Carry out a survey of the main industries in your area. As a class project, make a wallchart of your findings, dividing the industries into **primary**, **secondary** and **tertiary**.

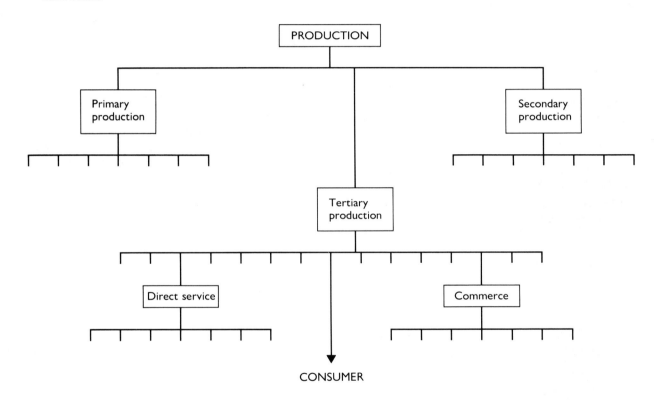

Fig. 1.3   Types of production

1.3 Specialisation

Any group of people must be able to produce goods and services if they are to survive. At a very basic level this means producing enough to feed, clothe and shelter themselves. If they had not been able to do this 'Stone Age man' would not have survived and the human race would have died out. Providing just enough to keep yourself alive is known as having a **subsistence economy**.

As time went on and people had learnt to cope with the necessities of life, they wanted more of the things that made life pleasant – in other words they wanted **luxuries**. They managed this by developing their methods of production – and their techniques of producing – so that they could produce more than they needed for their own use – a surplus. People swopped their surpluses to meet each other's needs. This was achieved through the development of the **division of labour**:

1 **By product** – instead of everyone hunting for their own food, building their own houses and making their own clothes, people concentrated on doing just one job, for example house building.

Fig. 1.4(A)   Bricklayer at work

Fig. 1.4(B)   Thatcher at work

2 **By process** – this took the division of labour one stage further. Instead of building a whole house, the jobs within it were divided up among different workers. One person would cut and assemble the stone, another would cut and fit the wood, another would thatch the roof . . .

This process of concentrating on one job is known as **specialisation**. Its advantages are:

(a) 'Practice makes perfect' – people gradually get better the more that they do something and so a better-quality product results.

(b) The more that you do a job the quicker you get at it, so more is produced in a given time, i.e. **productivity** rises.

There are disadvantages, however:

(a) Goods produced in this way will tend to be rather similar, particularly if they are made on machines; they lose their 'individuality'.

(b) It is extremely boring to do the same job every day. People become angry and frustrated and both their work and their welfare may suffer. One large firm used to have a room in which workers could go to smash china to relieve their feelings!

In most countries today firms which produce goods usually have a division of labour; goods are made in factories on a 'production line'. This is felt to be the most efficient way of producing goods and the one most likely to yield high output and profits. Recently, some firms have been trying to re-introduce a system in which each worker is responsible for making more, or even all, of the product, the idea being that they will be happier in their job – this is known as **job satisfaction**. They will then be more likely to work hard and less likely to cause disruption through absence and strikes. However, surveys that have been carried out to compare the two systems have found that there is little difference in productivity between them.

EXERCISE

1 Explain, in your own words, the meanings of the following terms and use them in a sentence to show you understand what they mean:
   (a) subsistence economy
   (b) necessity
   (c) luxury
   (d) surplus
   (e) division of labour by product
   (f) division of labour by process
   (g) specialisation
   (h) productivity

2 Explain, again in your own words, the advantages and disadvantages of the division of labour as a way of organising production.

3 Why are some firms moving away from a 'production line' method? Which method do *you* think is preferable? Explain your answer.

1.4 Money

It is important that we understand the part that money plays in business and the economy. The first thing that we need to work out is what money does *not* do.

■ Money is not worth anything in itself; a coin or a note is useless – *except for what it will buy.*
■ It does not measure the wealth of a country; only the goods and services produced by the country can do that.
■ It does not show how well a business is doing; a business can have a lot of cash but also a lot of bills and a falling order book.

Money is therefore only a representation of the goods and services produced in a country. If a lot more money is printed than there are goods and services to buy, then all that will happen is that the price level will rise. We will look more closely at this when we discuss inflation in Unit 7, Section 7.2.

So what *is* money? It is really a **token** that entitles the holder to a certain number of goods and services. It is needed to 'ration' them out because people have *unlimited wants* in terms of what they would *like* to have – a house in the country with a swimming pool in the garden, a large car, three holidays abroad per year, and so on – and the *limited means* available to meet those wants, i.e. there is only so much land, labour, capital, etc. In the very unlikely event of there being sufficient means to satisfy everyone's desires money would be unnecessary and people could just take what they wanted. Alas, that is just a dream!

At one time money did not exist. Instead people just swopped goods, a system known as **barter**. So you would go to market with your pig and perhaps swop it for the horse that you wanted. It does not take much imagination to see why this system proved unsatisfactory, however:

□ If the person with the horse did not want your pig a deal would not be possible – unless you had something else to offer. Barter needed a **mutual co-incidence of wants** to be successful.
□ You could not really divide up your pig. Goods are not **divisible**.
□ Nobody really knew how much anything was worth – is a pig worth just the same as a horse, or a little bit less, or a little bit more (see Fig. 1.5)? There was no **measure of value**.

Money avoids these problems for the following reasons:

■ It is **universally acceptable** within a country; it can be used to buy anything that is available, so removing the need for the mutual co-incidence of wants.

Fig. 1.5 Barter

■ It can be easily divided or multiplied into smaller or larger units.
■ It helps you to compare the value of goods.

Money has both **functions** – what it does – and **attributes** –what it is. Its **functions** can be summed up as follows:

■ It provides a means of exchange: it enables people to buy goods and services.
■ It provides a store of wealth: if held on to, it should maintain its value thus enabling people to save.

Its **attributes** can be summed up in the following ways:

■ Acceptability: people must be prepared to accept it as a means of payment.
■ Durability: it must be strong enough to survive being continually passed round.
■ Divisibility: it must be easily divided up into smaller units.
■ Portability: it must be easily carried.

Changes in the value of money

We mentioned that one of the functions of money was that it should act as a store of wealth. There are periods in which money will not hold its value, however, and that is known as **inflation**. In modern times most countries are affected by some rate of inflation and so the value of money steadily falls, but when the inflation rate is only a few percentage points each year it is barely noticeable. If prices of goods and services are rising it follows that the money in your pocket will pay for fewer of them, so its *value will be falling.*

This will particularly affect people on **fixed incomes**, such as pensioners, students and the unemployed. If you are in paid employment, however, you have the chance of getting a wage increase to keep up with price increases. It will also make **saving** less attractive, as the money saved will be able to buy less in the future. On the other hand, borrowing will be more attractive because when you pay it back it will be worth less. Of course, this will mean that people will be less willing to lend money, unless they can charge a rate of interest that compensates.

The value of money is measured in the **retail price index** which takes a typical 'basket of goods' and compares the price of the items over varying periods of time (see Fig. 1.6). It takes the average of these prices to estimate the inflation rate for the period.

EXERCISE

1 Explain, in your own words, why it is preferable to use money rather than barter for goods and services.

2 Why is money a 'ration of scarce goods'?

3 Write out and explain, in your own words, what money is and what it does.

4 Make out a table showing who are the **gainers** from falls in the value of money and who are the **losers**.

EXTENSION ACTIVITY
Research to find out exactly how the Retail Price Index is drawn up and write out a report on how it developed during the course of last year. Draw a graph showing the inflation rate, month by month, for that year.

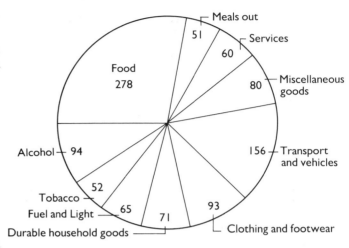

Fig. 1.6 Retail price index (early '80's)

1.5 Location

Where shall we place our business?

Imagine that you have discovered that everyone in your area would like to be able to buy fried fish and chips but there is nowhere that sells them. You realise that you could sell plenty so you decide to set up in business and sell fish and chips. The first thing that you will need to do, of course, is to find some money. You will need to buy a place to prepare your fish and chips – **premises**, and equipment with which to prepare them – **machinery**. (In later units we will consider how you could raise your money and what you would do with it.) We will now concentrate on the premises and how you would decide where the best place is – the **location**. Of course, in real life, land will not necessarily be available at an affordable rent in the 'perfect' location but it is still very useful to look at the general principles that would influence your choice.

The most important factor, especially if you are setting up in business for the first time, is that your premises must be convenient for those who are likely to use them – the **customers**. So there is little point in placing your fish and chip shop in a back street that nobody ever uses. You would have no customers and a lot of unsold fish and chips. You need to choose a location that people *know* about and are likely to use.

Your location must also be convenient for those who will supply you with the goods that you need to make the product – in this case fish and potatoes. Ideally, you would need to be near the sea and a potato field! Failing that, it is important for most businesses to be on or near a main road. It is going to be very expensive and inconvenient for your suppliers to bring you the goods if you are at the end of a ten-mile mud track in the middle of the hills.

Of course, whenever a business is set up it will have effects on people in the area – some good and some bad. The good effects are known as **social benefits**. Your fish and chip shop will obviously provide people with a product that was not available before – fish and chips cooked and ready to eat. If you are successful and find that you need to take on more people to work for you then you will be providing jobs, or **employment**, for people in the area. This will not only be good for them but they will have money to spend from the wages that you pay them and that will help other businesses in the area. Hopefully, your fish and chips may also be so good that people will come from miles around to sample them. They may spend money in other local shops and so give them a boost as well.

What about the bad effects – the **social costs**? The cooking of fish and chips produces a strong smell. People may not like the aroma when they walk down the street. Unfortunately people are not always very tidy – the newspaper or containers in which they ate the fish and chips may be littering the street. People are sometimes noisy when they are in large groups and local residents may be disturbed. All these factors need to be taken into account before a final decision can be made as to where the business is to be located.

Fig. 1.7   The importance of location

Nuclear Power Station

Look carefully at Fig. 1.8. There is a choice of three sites for a nuclear power station – Roxbridge, Moxbridge and Loxbridge. You will need the following information:

(a) Roxbridge has a population of 20,000. Ten per cent of the working population are unemployed and most of them are unskilled.
(b) Moxbridge has a population of 10,000. Just 1 per cent are unemployed but they are highly skilled.
(c) Loxbridge has a population of 500. They are all currently in work.
(d) Uranium necessary for producing nuclear power which has to be imported from overseas.

In making your decision as to the best site for the power station you must take the following factors into account:

A = Proximity to market
B = Convenience for suppliers
C = Minimise social costs
D = Maximise social benefits
E = Availability of suitable labour force

Copy and fill in the following table using a marking system of 1–5. For instance, if you think that Moxbridge is the most convenient location for suppliers place a 1 underneath **A** and beside **M**, etc.

Add up the total for each town. The town with the *smallest* total is the most suitable. Or is it? . . .

	A	B	C	D	E	Total
R						
M						
L						

EXTENSION ACTIVITY

Look at your result and think about whether you would have chosen this town just from looking at the map and thinking about it. If the two are different, think about *why*. Perhaps not all the factors that you were asked to take into account were of equal value. For instance, you might think that if you are dealing with nuclear power **safety** for the surrounding population is an over-riding consideration and so **minimising social costs** is the most important of all. How could you show this in your table? Discuss this with the class and your teacher and produce a second table that **weights** the different factors according to the importance that you put on them. Was it easy to reach agreement among yourselves or did you have to 'agree to differ'? Write an essay explaining your own choice.

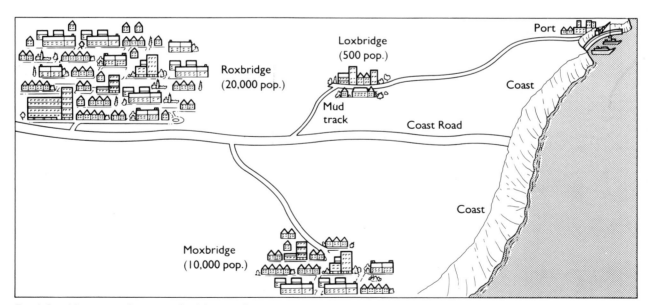

Fig. 1.8 Alternative locations for Magnox Power station

1.6 Government aid

An increasingly important factor in a firm's decision about where to locate is the level of **government** and **local authority aid** that is available. Look at the graph in Fig. 1.9.

It is quite obvious that some regions of the country have far higher levels of unemployment than others. List the different regions in order of unemployment, starting at the highest at the beginning of 1988, with the unemployment percentage beside each.

The effects on an area with high levels of unemployment are widespread. People have less money to spend in the shops so local business suffers. Government may be less concerned about the roads and schools in the area so the services offered worsen and there is even less incentive for firms to set up in the area. Some areas can be hit suddenly if an important local employer, such as a steel works, closes down.

Governments try to help such areas, partly because of the human suffering and waste that results from unemployment and partly because having pockets of very high unemployment **distorts** the whole economy, bringing down wages and house prices out of line with the rest of the country.

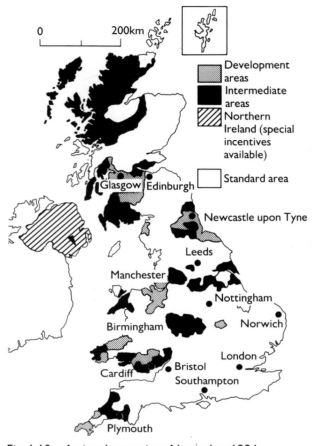

Fig. 1.10   Assisted areas since November 1984

Look at the map in Fig. 1.10. If you compare the areas of high unemployment seen in Fig. 1.9 with the shaded areas on the map, you will notice the similarity. There are two different shades:

1 **Development areas** – these are the areas of the highest unemployment and receive the most government assistance.
2 **Intermediate areas** – these are the areas where unemployment is still a cause for concern but is lower than development areas and so the aid given is less.

Grants and financial incentives

Encouragement to business is also given by local authorities. For example, North Tyneside Council in the north-east of England provides the following incentives to firms to move to the area:

■ three-month 'rent free' periods on lettings of council-owned factory units in certain places;
■ grants of up to £1,000 towards the costs of attending trade exhibitions;

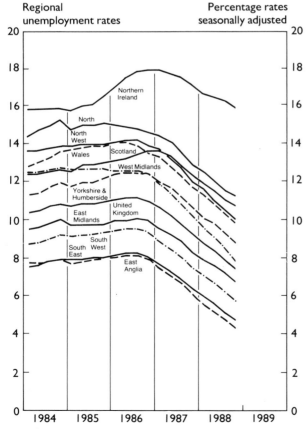

Fig. 1.9   Regional unemployment rates

- wage subsidies of £25 per week for 52 weeks for employers who recruit 16–24 year olds who have been unemployed for over six months;
- grants of up to £2,000 to help new businesses to start up and towards essential plant and equipment or building modifications for small businesses to expand;
- grants and loans of up to £1,000 towards the cost of setting up a co-operative;
- grant assistance of up to 75 per cent for building and environmental improvement works within certain areas;
- loans of up to £20,000 and grants of up to £10,000 made available to manufacturing and service industries. This aid is closely linked to the creation or retention of jobs.

Other forms of assistance provided in other areas include:

- interest relief on loans to buy capital equipment;
- exemption from paying any rates to the local authority for a certain period of time;
- business development loans which are often interest-free over the period of the loan – usually three years.

How effective are these measures?

The thinking behind all these measures is that businesses will be encouraged to locate in areas of high unemployment, thus bringing down the level of unemployment in that area. There are some people who say that this is a waste of money and that regional differences in unemployment will be 'ironed out' because wages will be lower in these areas and so firms will come without special grants. There is little evidence that this has

been the case; on the contrary, as we have already seen, high unemployment leads to worsening services and so even less incentive for firms to come.

So has the offer of various grants been any more effective? It is certainly possible to find specific cases where the offer of a grant has persuaded a firm to move to a particular area. The grants offered to Nissan, the Japanese car corporation, were very influential in persuading them to locate their new plant in Sunderland (see Unit 2, Section 2.5) and the Trustee Savings Bank was persuaded to move some of its offices from Hampshire to South Wales by the offer of financial help.

On the other hand, it cannot be denied that there are still wide differences in unemployment between different areas – largely to do with history: 'heavy industry' such as ship-building, steel production and mining have traditionally been located in the North of England and in Scotland and Wales and these industries are gradually dying because of international competition and reduced manpower needs. The new 'sunrise' industries such as computing and micro-electronics are overwhelmingly located in the South. Financial incentives have not yet proved sufficient to correct the balance.

EXERCISE

1 Explain in your own words the reasons why governments provide grants to industry in some regions. What different types of assistance are available?
2 How much government assistance has been provided in *your area*? Write a polite letter to your local council office asking for details. Write them up in the form of a short report.

2.1 The sole trader

Consider the following tale:

Dai Jones was a blast-furnaceman who was employed by the British Steel Corporation. As you may be aware, however, a number of steel plants have been closed in recent years as the corporation has tried to become more profitable. Unfortunately Dai's works was part of that process and, after 25 years, he was made redundant.

Dai was devastated. He had recently married (not before time, according to his mother!) and his wife had just borne their first child so she could not go to work and both needed supporting. The steel industry had been his life – it was the only job that he had ever had, and he did not want to work for anybody else. Anyway, what chance did he have of finding other work in a town that had been built around the steel industry and which now had a 20 per cent unemployment rate of men of employable age? The situation seemed desperate.

Dai was in a pub 'drowning his sorrows' one night when he started talking to a fellow from the other side of town whom he knew vaguely. 'You want to do the same as me, mate. I was in exactly the same position as you five years ago. I applied for hundreds of jobs and was up against hundreds of people each time. Then I suddenly thought "If they won't employ me, I'll employ myself!" I am a bit handy with cars so I put all my redundancy money plus some that I wheedled out of the bank into buying premises and basic equipment. Oh, it was tough at first, I'll grant you that, but the business took off and now I employ half a dozen mechanics, I don't get my hands dirty very often and I'm doing very nicely, thank you!'

This set Dai thinking. He wasn't much interested in cars and anyway there would obviously have been some competition in that area. He had always enjoyed 'DIY' however; only last year he had built rather a smart extension to his kitchen. What about setting up his own building firm? . . .

Dai thought over the matter for some weeks, discussed it with his wife, discussed it with his bank manager and eventually decided that his redundancy money plus a small bank loan could set him on the road. Having to take out the loan worried him – if the business failed how could he pay it back? As his only realistic chance of work seemed to be in London where the cost of housing was exorbitant and which was far from his beloved valleys, he felt that he had no choice.

One advantage of the building business was that he did not need to buy premises – he could work from home. His main investment was in tools and, to a lesser extent, advertising. The first few weeks were worrying – the advertisements in the shop windows seemed to attract little custom and he was idle for much of the time. He began to think that he had made a terrible mistake. Having committed himself this far he felt that he had to try everything and so he intensified his advertising campaign by leafleting houses in certain 'target areas'.

At first this did not seem to improve matters. Dai became very depressed. Working on his own meant that he did not really have anyone to discuss the problems with and that made it even worse. He had visions of selling his house to pay off his debts. One day the phone rang. It was a local millionaire (one of the few!). He wanted extensive work done on his house. He estimated that it would be about six weeks' work for one man – and he hinted that, if he was pleased with the result there could be more work coming Dai's way, both from him and also his friends.

That was the break that Dai needed. He satisfied the millionaire and a lot of work followed. Life was still not a garden of roses, however. Success also brought its problems. He found that he was working extremely long hours; there were books to keep, on top of the building work itself which he was, of course, doing all himself. Like any of us Dai was better at some aspects of his job than others. He did not like painting, for instance. This was eased when he managed to employ a lad, but between them they still had limited skill in certain areas and he lacked the finance to take on anybody else. He could not really discuss business affairs with his young workmate whose main interests were elsewhere, and he felt the responsibility for running the business acutely. Finally there was always at the back of his mind the knowledge that things could go wrong and if this happened he could be

---

POINTS FOR DISCUSSION

1 Explain the meaning of the following terms:
   (a) corporation
   (b) profitable
   (c) redundant
   (d) competition
2 Try to work out why British Steel felt that it had to close down plants to become more profitable.

3 Who owns British Steel?
4 Why do you think that the car repair business was doing so well?
5 If you were Dai, what considerations would you take into account when deciding whether to set up your building firm? What particular worries would you have?

forced to sell his house and all his possessions to pay off his debts. On the other hand, there was no doubting that he liked the independence of running the business himself; on good days it was great – nobody to consult, nobody to order him about. That was one aspect of the steel works that he definitely did *not* miss! What was also satisfying was being able to keep the profits that he earned.

EXERCISE

Go through the story again and pick out all the advantages and disadvantages that Dai found when working on his own. Are there any more that you can think of? Would *you* like to run your own business or would you rather work for someone else? Explain your reasons for your choice.

EXTENSION ACTIVITY

Find a sole trader in your area; it should not be difficult, as this is by far the most common form of business in the United Kingdom – small newsagents, builders, plumbers, electricians, etc. Perhaps one will be willing to talk to you about the way that they run their business and the 'pros and cons' of being a sole trader. You could tape it and then write it up. How closely do your findings correspond with the example above?

Fig. 2.1   Examples of sole traders

2.2 The partnership

Fig. 2.2 The benefits of a partnership

After working on his own for a couple of years Dai's business was now a 'growing concern'. He was never short of business and he had repaid all the money that he had borrowed from the bank. It was hard work but it was proving worthwhile. He felt that this was a good time to look for a partner. As it happened one of his friends, Elwyn Smith, had recently been made redundant from a local engineering factory; he was also quite handy with a hammer.

What could Elwyn offer the business? Well, there was his redundancy money – more **capital**; his expertise in various areas – more **specialisation**; his advice where needed – more **consultation**; and his security to place against any possible debts – **sharing of risks**.

What could the business offer Elwyn? Obviously a means of earning his livelihood, a share in any profits that were made and the chance to be part of an expanding business. However, he was also risking his own money and, indeed, all his possessions if things went wrong – as they always can in business.

Consultation is all very well but a partnership also provides somebody to argue with.

At first all went well and they worked together harmoniously. Elwyn thought that sound financial management was very important and so tended to look after the books on top of his share of the building work; this had never been Dai's strong point. At first Dai was delighted that there was someone to take the burden off him and Elwyn got the books into good order. He was very strict about what was spent by 'the company' and what was spent by Dai and himself. So there were arguments over small issues such as who should pay for the tea-bags. Dai thought that it was a legitimate 'perk' while Elwyn insisted that they were for personal rather than business use and so should not be paid for out of business funds.

Many of the problems that they faced could be traced back to the fact that they had not formed any 'partnership agreement' or **Articles of Partnership** when they initially got together. This would cover such issues as:

- how much capital is provided by each of the partners;
- how profits are to be shared and losses to be borne;
- whether there is to be any payment for working on a partnership business;
- how disputes are to be settled;
- how decisions are to be arrived at, disputes solved and management tasks to be distributed.

FOR DISCUSSION

If you were Elwyn Smith, what factors would you take into account before deciding whether to become a partner or not? If you were Dai Jones, how would you decide whether to have Elwyn as a partner? Write a dialogue between the two while the subject is being discussed. You could act it out in front of the class in the form of an interview.

EXERCISE

Dai and Elwyn spent a lot of time discussing their partnership agreement. Using the list of issues given, draw up a Contract of Partnership for Dai and Elwyn.

For each problem think of the fairest way of solving it. For instance, if Dai has put in double the money that Elwyn has it might be fairer if he were to receive double share of any profits.

Head your document:

Contract of Partnership

Partnership agreement between Dai Jones and Elwyn Smith of . . .

Although we are dealing with a partnership of two people in this case – as the term 'partnership' perhaps implies – this form of business organisation is not necessarily restricted to two members. Originally partnerships could have between two and twenty members. The limit of twenty was laid down by the **Partnership Act (1890)** to prevent partnerships from becoming too large and difficult to control. It was a difficult limit to enforce however, and partnerships still had **unlimited liability**, which meant they risked losing all their money and possessions if the business failed.

To try to get round these problems the **Limited Partnership Act (1907)** was introduced. This brought in the **sleeping partner** who would contribute only money but would play no part in the management of the business. In return they received **limited liability** which means that in the event of bankruptcy they would lose only the money that they had invested in the company; their possessions would be safe. Partnerships could now, in certain circumstances, have up to 200 members – as long as at least one was an ordinary partner as opposed to a sleeping partner and so could take responsibility for all the debts.

The main difficulty that Dai and Elwyn faced as a partnership – even with their partnership agreement – was that they needed to reach agreement on all important decisions and that decisions taken by one partner are binding on the others whether they agree to them or not. For example, on one occasion Dai agreed to do a job on a Sunday, forgetting what a devout church-goer Elwyn was. He could not do the job without his partner and even though Elwyn was furious he had to go along as Dai had made the 'contract' on his behalf also.

ACTIVITY

A partnership need not necessarily involve a business activity. It can involve two, or more, people in any kind of situation. The principles are basically the same.

Imagine that you are going on a walking expedition with a partner through the Himalayas. It will obviously require teamwork to get through and you will want to share the work and responsibility as equally as possible. In pairs, discuss all that you will need to purchase before you go, how you will finance it and all the tasks that will need to be carried out on the expedition itself. Draw up a 'Partnership Agreement' for your trip and set it out in a similar way to the agreement for Dai and Elwyn.

2.3 The limited company

The private limited company

Time passed and the business grew. Dai and Elwyn were employing thirty people and they had a smart office on the edge of town. They had taken on a couple more partners, one of whom was very interested in design. This meant they could expand the range of services that they could offer and they were thinking very seriously of entering the house-building business. A few problems held them back, however; the 'decision-making' structure of the business was still rather vague and it was never clear who had the 'final say'. Usually they reached agreement but Dai, in particular, could not help feeling that something a bit more 'formal' was necessary if they were to expand into a new market. They also needed an injection of new capital to buy the equipment that they would need. A few friends said that they might be interested in putting money in, but they would want to have some say in the running of the business and a share of the profits while keeping limited liability. There was a further worry; house building is a risky business. Accidents can happen to workers on site and the slightest error while the house is being built can cause problems later which could lead the new owners to take the builders to court. As long as the business was a partnership Dai, Elwyn and the other two partners could be held personally liable for any accident or errors.

All these considerations led them to form a new type of business – a **private limited company**. This would solve several of their problems in the following ways:

1 The problem of **decision making** is tackled by the creation of a **Board of Directors** headed by a **Managing Director**.
2 People will be encouraged to put **money** into the business because they will be given **shares** entitling them to have a say in the running of the company and a share in any profits that might be earned. It is shareholders who elect the Board of Directors. All shareholders have limited liability and so are in no danger of having to sell personal possessions to pay off any debts that the company may incur.
3 When a private limited company is formed a process called **incorporation** takes place. This means that the company acquires a 'separate legal identity' from its owners. So if there is an accident on site the injured party can take **the company** to court rather than its owners and the company, rather than Dai or Elwyn or any of the others, will have to pay any costs that might arise. This is why *all* members of a limited company can have limited liability; the debts are the company's and not its owners'. It also means that the company can have **continuity**. If a sole trader or a partner dies the company is dissolved because the company and the owners are one and the same thing and so, in effect, the company has 'died' also. If it is to carry on it has to be 're-formed' by its new owners. In a limited company, however, if one of the owners dies or leaves the company it just carries on and the shares can easily be transferred to somebody else.

When they decided to become a private limited company the first thing that Dai and Elwyn had to do was to **register** it with the **Registrar of Companies**. This involved giving certain information and the submission of certain documents:

■ **The Memorandum of Association**
This shows how the company will conduct itself in relation to the outside world. The following example is an abbreviated version:
 (a) The **name** of the company is Build-Anything Ltd.
 (b) The **objective** of the company is to engage in any form of building work that it might be asked to, subject to its ability to carry out the work.
 (c) The **registered address** of the company will be 25 Bledwyn Street, Gwent.
 (d) The liability of the shareholders is limited.
 (e) The company is to be a private limited company.
 (f) The **share capital** of the company is £50,000 divided into 50,000 shares of £1.

■ **The Articles of Association**
These are the internal rules of the company. They will cover such issues as voting rights for shares, arrangements for shareholders' meetings, the job of the directors, and so on.

When these, and one or two other information details have been submitted and a registration fee has been paid, Build-Anything Ltd will be handed its **Certificate of Incorporation** and will now legally exist. One thing that Dai and Elwyn have been told is that they can only sell shares to their friends or people that have been introduced to them – that is, on a private basis. (Hence the name, *private* limited company. They *cannot* offer their shares for sale on the Stock Exchange or advertise them in any way. If they wish to restrict the sale of shares to a particular family or group, this restriction must be included in the Articles of Association.

EXERCISE

1 Explain the statement 'the decision-making structure . . . was still rather vague' in the first paragraph.
2 Summarise, in your own words, the reasons why Dai and Elwyn decided to form a private limited company.
3 Explain why the concept of Incorporation is so important in solving the problems that Dai and Elwyn were facing.

4 Distinguish briefly between the functions of the Memorandum of Association and the Articles of Association.
5 Imagine you are a member of a partnership that wishes to expand. Write a note to one of your fellow partners explaining the advantages of becoming a private limited company.

The public limited company

The 'final step' in business ownership in the **private sector**, that is, owned by private individuals in one of the forms we have been looking at, is to become a **public limited company (PLC)**. All that has been stated about private limited companies applies also to public limited companies – with one very important exception. A public limited company *can* advertise its shares and it *can* sell them on the Stock Exchange. Following from this it needs to issue an additional document on registration – the **Prospectus** – which tells the public about the company and explains why the directors believe people should buy its shares. As a result of the 1980 Companies Act both types of limited company now must have a minimum of two shareholders with no maximum number – although, for obvious reasons, a PLC is unlikely to be anywhere near the minimum. There are other small differences: for example, a private limited company (Ltd) need only have one director who can carry on to whatever age he or she likes, while a public limited company (PLC) must have at least two directors who must retire when they are seventy years old – unless the shareholders decide otherwise. There are about 15,000 PLCs and 500,000 Ltds in this country. Obviously the total capital of the PLCs is much greater than that of the Ltds due to their greater size.

2.4 The public sector

Nationalisation v. privatisation

Around 90 per cent of industry in Britain is in the **private sector** – that is to say that it is owned by private individuals in one of the forms that we have just looked at. It is reasonable to assume that the main aim in these businesses is to make a profit for the owner, partners or shareholders.

The remaining 10 per cent, however, is owned by the government. When the government takes over an industry that was privately owned it is said to have been **nationalised**. Most nationalisation in Britain took place just after the Second World War and included industries such as the coal industry, the steel industry and the railways.

Recently the trend has been reversed and during the 1980s the Conservative government **privatised** a number of industries, i.e. sold them back from state ownership to the private sector. Examples include British Telecom, British Gas and British Airways.

Whether firms should be owned by the government or by individuals is a controversial issue. It divides people on **political** lines. As a general rule supporters of the Conservative Party tend to be against nationalisation and in favour of privatisation, while members of the Labour Party tend to oppose privatisation and some are in favour of even more nationalisation. Witness the following conversation in Dai and Elwyn's 'local':

Dai: Well, I have to admit it, this government is going about things well. I have been a Labour man all my life when I was working in the steelworks but Maggie is right. Even if you lose your job you can do well for yourself by getting off your backside and forming your own business. Look at us. We started with our redundancy money and now we have a flourishing building firm that is diversifying into new areas and selling shares. If we can do it anyone can. Now we are using some of the money that we have earned to buy shares in the companies that the government is privatising. I could make £2,000 on my Telecom shares if I sold them tomorrow.

Tommy: Look, it's all very well for you. I am not denying that you have worked hard and I am very pleased that things have worked out so well for you, but don't go round saying that 'anyone' could do it. If every employed person in this town tried to set up a building firm there wouldn't be enough business for any of them – and that goes for any other type of business. It is up to the government to create jobs by putting money into areas like this to help firms develop and also by nationalising more firms instead of selling them off so that people like you can make a quick killing on the shares; and they will make their employees jobless if necessary to make the firm profitable so that you get your dividend. If the government took over firms, they could run them to satisfy people's needs instead of making a profit – and that would include providing more jobs.

Dai: You're living in another world, sonny. Look at the firms that have been nationalised. Take the National Coal Board. I don't think that they have made a profit since 1945 – and it's all very well for you to say that profits are not important, but if the Coal Board makes a loss who has to cover it? You and me in our taxes, that's who. The miners are always striking – it was for a year last time – and they know that the government is always likely to bail out a nationalised industry; although this one has shown that it is not prepared to, thank goodness. Like all nationalised industries the Coal Board is a monopoly so if you don't like the service you can't go anywhere else. Have you ever tried to arrange for the Electricity Board to come round and do a repair at a time that suits you? There is so much bureaucracy and red tape that you can never speak to the right person and decision making is really slow. Their size also means that their workers do not really identify with the firm or feel part of it. With privatisation workers can buy shares in the company and so they have a real stake in the company performing well . . .

Tommy: Hang on a minute. Don't get too carried away. Just tell me how much more competition there is now for British Telecom, say – and everyone knows how much worse the service has become since it was privatised and they have simply been after more and more profits . . .

Dai: Well, there is Mercury in competition . . .

Tommy: Only for business calls, not domestic ones which really affect you and me.

Dai: Well, I don't know about that, but what's so wrong with profits, anyway? Where else are you going to get your funds from to invest in firms, to build new premises, to buy modern machinery, to employ more workers? How else are you going to know which investment programmes are worth undertaking and which are not unless you use profitability as your yardstick? Just think of all the investment that could take place in the new 'sunrise' industries such as micro-electronics and computing with all the jobs that could be created with the money that has been given to the Coal Board to keep open for just a few more years a few old, depleted and clapped out pits? Privatisation exposes firms to the real world where you stand or fall by your own efforts.

Tommy: What a nice picture you paint! If only it was actually like that. Unemployment does not seem likely to fall below 2 million with policies like this – and you know as well as I do that the 'sunrise' industries are capital intensive and don't create many new jobs. Anyway, most of them are concentrated in the South of England. If we had a government that was prepared to nationalise a large portion of the economy and increase public spending, jobs could soon be created. The government would just have

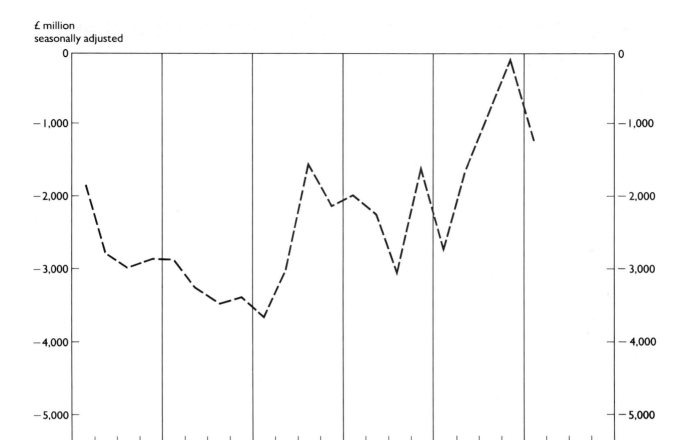

£ million
seasonally adjusted

Fig. 2.3 The loss made by public corporations 1983–88

to make it a priority over, say, making profits. Business would be able to concentrate on providing a good service for consumers and good working conditions for its employees. The government would be able to make a plan for the whole economy that would provide what people need – schools, houses and hospitals. Resources could be concentrated on the poorest areas – the inner cities, Wales, the North of England and Scotland. Enough wealth would be created to finance investment. Profits often just line people's pockets. What would happen to the railway service if British Rail were privatised? I'll tell you – the country lines which are not profitable would be closed down and people in country areas would be stranded . . . Anyway, what are you drinking?

EXERCISE

Read through the dialogue above and then make a list of the arguments for and against nationalisation. Divide your page in two; head one side *Arguments for Privatisation* and the other *Arguments for Nationalisation* and pick out as many as you can from the dialogue, putting them into the appropriate column. Can you think of any more that have not been mentioned? Which side of the argument do you support? Write a short essay with your answer explaining why. Your class could organise a debate to argue out the issue.

2.5 Multinational companies

A 'multinational' company is a business that operates in more than one country. To take a well-known example, the FORD motor company, founded in 1899 by Henry Ford in Detroit, USA, was established in Canada in 1903. In 1911 the company built a factory in England and in 1913 they established themselves in France. By 1920 they had plants in twenty countries covering Europe, Australia, South America, Japan, South Africa and India. Look at Fig. 2.4. The table gives the value of foreign investment by companies in various countries in three years: 1914, 1971 and 1978.

Fig. 2.4 **Foreign investments of the principal countries in the world (1914–78)**

Home country	Breakdown by percentage		
	1914	*1971*	*1978*
United Kingdom	45.5	14.8	11.9
West Germany	10.5	4.6	8.2
Switzerland	–	5.9	7.2
France	12.2	4.6	3.9
Netherlands	–	2.5	6.1
Sweden	–	1.5	1.6
Belgium-Luxemburg	–	1.5	1.2
Italy	8.7	1.9	0.9
Total Europe	*76.9*	*37.3*	*41.0*
United States	18.5	51.7	43.5
Japan	0.1	2.7	6.9
Canada	1.0	4.1	3.5
Total	*96.5*	*95.8*	*94.9*
Other countries (estimate)	3.5	4.2	5.1
General total	*100.0*	*100.0*	*100.0*
General total in billions of dollars	14.3	160.2	386.2

EXERCISE

Using Fig. 2.4, answer the following:
1 Which country had the largest percentage of foreign investment: (a) in 1914; (b) in 1978?
2 In which country was there the biggest fall in foreign investment between those years?
3 Which country had the smallest percentage of foreign investment in 1978?
4 Show these results graphically. Draw a **bar chart** comparing the countries in 1914 and a **pie chart** for the 1978 figures.

Why have multinational companies developed?

The following are possible reasons *why* there are multinational companies:

- The companies have been growing and wish to find new markets.
- Transport costs are reduced if companies produce in the countries where they wish to sell their goods.
- They provide employment and prosperity in the countries where they locate.
- They can search for the most 'favourable' conditions in which to produce.
- They can employ labour at a cheap rate if they locate in the 'right' country.
- They help the economies of the 'under-developed' countries if they locate there.

EXERCISE

Discuss the reasons given for the existence of multinational companies as if *you* were a director of one such company and place them in 'rank order' of importance for you. It might help you to give each a mark out of 10 and order them in that way.

Problems with multinational companies

Multinational companies also bring problems. These include the following:

- They may use their size and power to interfere in the running of the countries where they locate.
- They represent a reduction in 'national independence' for those countries.
- They may pay low wages and 'exploit' the workforce.
- They may use their position to 'dump' sub-quality products on those countries – a recent alleged example is powdered baby milk in Africa.
- Because they provide local competition, they may cause unemployment in other industries and also discourage the development of new industry.
- The **repatriation of profits** (profits sent back to the country where the company's main headquarters are) is bad for the balance of payments of the host country.

EXERCISE

Discuss the problems that multinational companies may bring in a similar way to the advantages – this time as if you were the Prime Minister of a host country. On balance do you think that multinational companies are a 'good thing'?

Nissan in Sunderland

Nissan Motor Company was formed in 1933 and quickly became one of Japan's leading motor manufacturers. It now has a world-wide production of 2.8 million cars per year, assembly plants in 24 countries and manufacturing plants in 21 countries. The company first came to the United Kingdom in 1968 when a handful of Datsun cars were sold by the newly-formed Datsun UK – an independent company set up to market and distribute the vehicles in Britain. In 1969, the first full year of sales, 1,200 vehicles were sold; in 1984 sales topped 1 million. In February of that year an agreement was signed with the British government to build a car plant in Sunderland, Tyne and Wear. Nissan gave the following explanation for choosing Britain:

'Nissan's decision to choose Britain for its European manufacturing base is closely linked with its strong presence in this country in terms of market share and also with the Japanese company's long association with the British motor industry, which goes back to 1934 when Nissan Motor Company first started producing Austin Seven cars under licence.'

In April 1985 the company signed an agreement with the Amalgamated Engineering Union (AEU), under which the AEU is the only union recognised at the plant. The reasons given for this 'single union' agreement are that they offer common terms and conditions to all employees and that a single union provides greater flexibility to employees concerning working practices. The agreement made included no 'clocking-on' for any employee, annual salaries for all employees to be paid monthly into bank

Fig. 2.5   Nissan team meeting area

accounts and the establishment of a Company Council on which representatives of all employees covered by the agreement sit together with management for consultations and negotiations.

The plant was opened in September 1986. In the first year production levels rose to 29,000 units per annum and 300 full-time jobs were created a year ahead of schedule. Total employment in 1988 was 1,600.

Fig. 2.6   Nissan car body shop robot welding

EXERCISE

1 What effect do you think the increase in sales of Nissan cars in the United Kingdom between 1968 and 1984 had on the British car industry?

2 Pick out Nissan's reasons for locating in Britain and try and think of some others that they did not mention – particularly bearing in mind that they located in Sunderland.

3 Why are 'single union' agreements more convenient for management?

4 What other unions might have wanted to be involved at Nissan and what would you expect their reaction to be to the agreement?

5 What do you think were the company's reasons for including in the agreement the points mentioned in the extract?

6 Using the information given here in earlier sections, draw up a table showing the advantages and disadvantages for the United Kingdom of Nissan building their plant in Sunderland.

7 The newspaper article below sets out the various sites that Nissan chose from. Pick out the advantages and disadvantages that you can find out about each of the *three favourite* sites – Newport, North Killingholme and Sunderland Airport. Make a careful note of the level of **grant** that was available for each.

Although Nissan has a complete dossier on the eight sites which comprised the original short-list of possible locations for its UK plant, it is believed the company will visit each one again in the next few weeks to bring its information up to date.

It is also expected that the eight will be reduced to a smaller, final short-list and that these will receive a second visit in which more detailed questions of site, infrastructure, communications and availability of labour will be discussed.

It is still open for the company to add locations to its file, but given the time available before a decision is made – the company has said it will announce the site before the end of March – it is thought unlikely to go outside the eight.

Of the eight, three sites emerged as favourites the last time around: Llanwern, just outside Newport in South Wales; North Killingholme airfield, near Immingham in South Humberside and Sunderland airport.

The first two are in development areas and the third in a special development area. By choosing the Sunderland site Nissan would be automatically entitled to 22 per cent grants towards the cost of all new buildings and plant. In the other two sites it would get 15 per cent grants.

In addition it will almost certainly qualify for selective financial assistance under section 7 of the 1972 Industry Act. This package alone could amount to as much as £35m.

The three favourites are:

NEWPORT: The site lies between the M4 and the coast and backs on to British Steel's Llanwern works. BSC owns nearly 500 acres of the land.

However, since the original short-list was drawn up, South Wales has been hit by traffic restrictions on the Severn Bridge. Any amelioration is unlikely for at least five years. The nearest docks at Newport are approximately three miles away.

NORTH KILLINGHOLME: This comprises an airport site with some 4,000 acres available just north of the A18. The road has recently been rebuilt to motorway standards and extended into Grimsby. It links directly to the M18, and the national motorway network, and across the Humber Bridge.

Although the site is owned by seven private holders two of them have 800 acres each, the amount originally needed by the company. The nearest docks are at Immingham about three miles away and at Grimsby approximately 10 miles distant.

SUNDERLAND AIRPORT: The land here is in four hands but two of them are the new town and Tyne and Wear County Council. The site is to the east of the A1 (M) and convenient to the steelworks on Teesside to the south.

Closest docks are at Sunderland at about two to three miles away.

The other sites are:

STOCKTON: An area at Ingleby Barwick, south of Thornaby near the A19 and next to the Teesside industrial estate. Some 1,750 acres are available, largely in the hands of one developer. Nearest docks are at Teesside.

There is a second site in the area west of Eaglescliffe and south of a new section of the A66 with 1,200 acres available, in three or four hands. The nearest docks again are at Teesside.

STALLINGBOROUGH: A site of over 800 acres, near to the other South Humberside location, north of the A18 and mainly in the hands of two land owners. Nearest docks are at Immingham and Grimsby.

CARDIFF: A small site of 230 acres at Wentloog owned by the County Council between the M4 and the coast with another 710 acres likely to be available. There is a good pool of labour available and the nearest docks are at Cardiff.

SHOTTON: This comprises a site on Deeside, where some 1,800 acres are available. It is the farthest of the sites from the motorway network but nearest to main component suppliers. The closest docks are at Ellesmere Port.

2.6 Co-operatives

A **co-operative** is a way of running a business that is different from the methods used in either the private or public sectors. Its basic principle is that **the people working in the business own it and run it**. There are really two types of co-operative:

1 The retail co-operative

As the name suggests, this is where the *selling* of goods or services is run on co-operative lines. The best-known example is that of the **co-operative stores** which can be seen all over the country. The Co-operative Society was founded in the mid-nineteenth century by a group of working men in Rochdale, Lancashire, who felt that the prices charged by the stores of the time were too high. So they got together and formed a society whose main aim was to sell goods cheaply rather than make high profits. Because they all had an equal share in the society, they also shared equally in any profits that were made. As the business grew, all the customers of the society's stores were given a chance to become members.

This system continues today, and at the end of each year all members receive a **dividend** based on the amount of money that they have spent in the store during the course of the year. They also have the right to attend the **Annual General Meeting** of the co-operative and vote on the policy that should be followed.

2 The producer co-operative

This type of co-operative became popular in England during the 1970s, when unemployment started to rise. It is formed when a group of workers in a factory, or any other place of work, get together and take over the running of the business. It was seen by many workers as the only way of avoiding redundancy when their employers wanted to close down a workplace. Consider the following imaginary example.

Tonto Toys Ltd

Tonto Toys Ltd made soft, cuddly bears. They had suffered a large fall in sales over a number of years, however, and in time found themselves in the hands of the receiver. The 150 employees were warned that they would shortly have to seek alternative employment. A number of them were convinced that there *was* a viable business, however, and that more vigorous selling could transform the situation for the company. The management was not prepared to try, so the employees decided that they should have a go.

The only way in which they could take control of the situation was by forming a co-operative – and that is what they proceeded to do. They called a meeting of the workforce and obtained everyone's agreement. More than that, they each agreed to invest £500 of their redundancy pay to set the wheels of the new business in motion.

The main problem that they faced was funding: a number of financial institutions that they approached seemed to regard the workers' co-operative as a 'bad risk' and were reluctant to provide them with loans. Eventually they managed to persuade one of the commercial banks to help out, but not to the extent that they needed – and at what appeared to them to be a high rate of interest in comparison with other loans that the bank made. The local council gave them some help with the costs of removal into new premises, but little else.

The co-operative managed to rebuild a viable business through the personal commitment of the members – in terms of time *and* money. Some of them were even prepared to be personally liable for the loans taken out. In three years the workforce expanded by twenty and the turnover rose by 20 per cent. As one of the problems of the old business was a 'saturation' of the cuddly bears market, they have since diversified their activities and now produce dolls and 'action men' toys which appear to sell more successfully. As one of the elected directors says, 'Whatever type of business you are in, you still have to carry out your market research and be flexible enough to respond to any results that you find.'

Life never becomes easy for members of a co-operative. They are always struggling to compete against established firms and to win acceptance from financial institutions. The members still feel that they were let down by the banks and that they have stayed afloat *despite* rather than because of them. For instance, this unwillingness to give greater financial support is making it difficult for them to develop export markets as they would like to do. However, the members recognise that the alternative for them is redundancy and that thought motivates them to continue.

EXERCISE

1 What motivated the workers to form a co-operative at Tonto Toys?
2 Why could they not have proceeded without calling a meeting of the workforce?
3 How did the workforce demonstrate their commitment to the venture?
4 Why do you think that the bank charged them a relatively high rate of interest?
5 Explain, in your own words, the marketing strategy of the co-operative.
6 Why was the director 'elected'?
7 Why might they be especially keen to develop export markets?
8 Do you think that they are entitled to feel let down by the banks and other financial institutions? Write a short speech that one of the co-operative members might make expressing such a feeling and a reply that the Bank Manager might pen.

2.7 How co-operatives are run

We saw in the last section how co-operatives have sometimes been set up when a place of work has been faced with closure and the workers have taken it over and tried to run it themselves to avoid redundancy. It is worth looking in a little more detail at how co-operatives are actually run and how this varies from running the 'normal' company, because some people think that this method is better.

A co-operative is run in a more '**democratic**' way than other companies. Instead of just one person – or a small Board of Directors – taking all the decisions, everyone has a say. What this means is that instead of 'ultimate responsibility' resting with the Sole Trader, Partners or Managing Director, it is a **general meeting** of all members that has the 'final say' on any decision and has to take the consequences. Obviously it is not possible for a large general meeting to take all the decisions on a 'day-to-day' basis; this is done by a **committee** that is elected by the general meeting.

In any business there are many jobs to be carried out and in a co-operative the committee will usually draw up a **rota** of tasks. In some co-operatives there is **job rotation** which means that everybody takes a turn at each job. This has the advantage of giving variety to all workers and allowing them to see how each part of the business works; thus it is likely to reduce boredom and increase interest.

On the other hand, it does reduce the benefits of 'specialisation' (see Unit 1, Section 1.3) and some jobs may take so much training that it is not possible to rotate them regularly. Each co-operative will have a **Secretary** who will deal with all the *legal* issues and a **Treasurer** who deals with the money. These are often rotated also – but not usually more than once a year.

One other area in which there is a great difference between co-operatives and other firms is in the differences in wages between different jobs – **wage differentials**. As you probably know, in most businesses there is a great difference between the wages of the managers and the workers – particularly if the workers are unskilled. The argument is that nobody would be prepared to take the responsibility of helping to run a business if they did not receive a lot more than if they just worked in it. In a co-operative the 'starting point' is the idea that *all* jobs are equally necessary – from the general labourer to the manager – and so they should be paid either the same or with only a small differential. This can cause problems in recruiting people of 'high calibre' but many people of talent are prepared to work for less in a co-operative because they feel they are part of the business and have a say in its development, and because they 'believe in its ideals'.

Fig. 2.7   Job rotation in a co-operative

Fig. 2.8 Suma's best selling product

Triangle Wholefoods Collective (SUMA)

Suma is a wholefood wholesaling outlet that now has an annual turnover of £4½ million. It was started in 1975 with approximately £4,000 capital. Its membership has increased from seven to forty. Its area stretches from Leeds up to Newcastle and across to Hull and Manchester, Nottingham and Lincoln, with goods coming in from London. The work of the co-operative involves buying and marketing, warehousing and driving as well as office administration. Warehouse work and some of the office administration is rotated daily, along with the driving jobs. There are also specialised areas of work where continuity is needed over a period of time. These include buying, purchase and customer accounts, transport management and marketing. These jobs are rotated over a two-year period with two people at a time working on the job. These people still work one or two days a week in the warehouse, or driving or doing the more routine office administration.

Decisions used to be made at weekly Wednesday meetings, but as the number of members grew this was found to be too unwieldy and now the co-op has been divided into three sections, roughly corresponding with work areas, which meet on separate days to discuss current issues. All decisions are reached by **consensus** (the majority view that comes over in the discussion). These decisions are co-ordinated by a **hub**, consisting of a representative from each sector, plus the Finance Officer and the Personnel Officer.

The only difference in pay is for members with dependants who get an extra allowance for each dependant. The co-operative aims to provide facilities which are much better than those in a conventional work-place. At the time of writing, the age range of people working for the co-operative is between early 20s and 40s.

In 1976 Suma set up a wholefood retail shop, Beano, in Leeds. This was supported financially by Suma in its early months but became a completely independent co-operative in 1978. Other co-operatives have been set up by ex-Suma members, including a real-ale off-licence and a food packaging service directly linked to Suma. This underlines the fundamental principle of the business as it grows: that as far as possible it will seek to establish other enterprises as independent co-operatives. Suma has a 'social objective' written into its constitution. All members have agreed that whenever they give themselves a pay rise they will put the same amount per member into a **co-operative loan fund**. This fund lends money interest free for six months and then at a low interest rate to new or expanding co-operatives in need of financial assistance.

EXERCISE

Read the passage about Suma carefully and pick out all the differences that you can find between the way that it is run and the way of running other types of business. You could write this in the form of an essay. With each difference that you find put down all the advantages and disadvantages that you can think of for the co-operative way of doing things.

EXTENSION ACTIVITY

Research to find out what businesses in your area are run as co-operatives (your local library or town hall may have the information you need). Write a polite letter to one of them asking for information about how the business is run and whether a small group from your class could visit and interview some members. You could make this a topic for a **project** – prepare a list of questions you could ask and report back to the class on your findings.

2.8 Franchising

Franchising occurs when the owner of a successful business grants somebody else the **licence** to market its product. The owner of the business is called the **franchisor**; the person who obtains a licence to sell the product is called the **franchisee**. The franchisee usually pays both an initial fee and a royalty on sales. An example of this arrangement is the Body Shop. It opens branches in towns and advertises for people to run them. They pay an initial fee and a share of their profits to the Body Shop; the rest of what they earn, they keep.

In many ways the franchisee is like a sole trader – without much of the risk. He or she can take advantage of the market and public awareness already created by the 'parent firm' and will also benefit from their management experience, financial backing, marketing strategy, etc. On a day-to-day basis the franchisee has to run the concern on his or her own behalf, however – just like a sole trader. The franchisor, on the other hand, finds it an easy way to expand and create a national presence through developing 'agents' in large numbers of towns. Assuming that the concerns are successful the franchisor will earn income as well.

There are three main types of franchise:

1 **Job franchise** provides a service – hairdressing, plumbing, etc.
2 **Business format franchise** – an example of this is the Body Shop which we have already mentioned. It covers sales from retail outlets.
3 **Investment franchise** involves an agreement with a company rather than an individual and covers such operations as hotel chains.

Fig. 2.9   An example of business format franchise

At the end of 1987 there were 15,000 franchised outlets belonging to 250 franchising businesses. Annual turnover has increased from £1 billion in 1984 to over £3.1 billion at the end of 1987, and is anticipated to reach £7.7 billion in 1992. Between them, franchises employ over 169,000 people, compared with 9,000 in 1984, and 98 per cent of franchisees operating in established franchises are successful. Fig. 2.10 compares the situation in the UK with other countries.

	UK	USA	Canada	France
Population in millions	56	235	22	55
Sales total (£ billions)	2	94	11	6
Sales per capital (£000s)	36	400	440	100

Fig. 2.10   **Franchising in different countries**

The British Franchise Association

The British Franchise Association (BFA) is a body that represents 'responsible' franchising, and covers an expanding area of British business, including fast food, retailing, automobile and commercial services. The association's main aim is to establish 'a clear definition of the ethical franchising standards to assist members of the public, press, potential investors and government bodies in differentiating between sound business opportunities and any suspect investment offers'. In other words, the association is trying to work out **rules** for the proper running of franchises and has drawn up a code of **business practice** that all BFA members must follow. It also encourages its members to exchange information and ideas.

Interest in franchising is still increasing and the National Franchise Exhibition is now an established and successful annual event. It takes place in London during October and in 1988 featured 140 exhibitors and catered for over 14,000 visitors. Seminars are held during the exhibition, attended both by business people interested in expanding their own businesses through franchising and by those interested in running franchise businesses.

International growth

The USA is the leading nation in world franchising; Canada and Japan are rapidly following its example.

In Europe the United Kingdom is in close company with France, Belgium and Sweden in the rate of development of franchise networks. As far as foreign franchisors in the UK are concerned, the USA is the most important and Belgian companies are next.

EXERCISE

1 Research to find out which of the businesses shown in Fig. 2.11 are run as franchises.
2 Write a short essay on 'The development of franchising in the United Kingdom'. You will need to include the following points:
  (a) a clear definition of franchising;
  (b) the different types of franchise;
  (c) the advantages for franchisor and franchisee;
  (d) the facts which point to its continued growth;
  (e) the role of the BFA.

ACTIVITY

Devise a questionnaire that you could use to ask franchisees about the benefits and problems of franchising. Visit your nearest shopping centre to find which shops are run on a franchise. Where the answer is 'Yes' ask the owners if they would be prepared to answer your questionnaire. What proportion of shops in the centre are franchised?

    Make a list of the names of franchise companies that you come across and compare it with the lists of others in your group or class. Do the same names appear on several lists? Write a polite letter to a firm that sells franchises and ask for their views on franchising. This could make a good project.

Fig. 2.11   Selection of businesses seen in the highstreet

2.9 Joint ventures

When two (or more) businesses join together to carry out a project, this is called a **joint venture**. There are three main areas where businesses can help each other:

1 access to markets;
2 finance;
3 expertise in various areas.

The best way to appreciate the advantages that such an arrangement can offer is to look at a 'real-life' example.

Austin Rover/Honda

After the Second World War there was a tremendous growth in car sales; before the war motor cars had been a 'luxury' enjoyed by only a few of the more wealthy families, while in the thirty or so years after the war they gradually became available to the majority of families. All of the main car companies in the world enjoyed rising sales and profits. Things began to change in the 1970s, however – mainly due to the greatly increased price of oil after 1972 which, of course, made petrol much more expensive and also affected industry throughout Western Europe, causing higher unemployment and so lower car sales.

This caused the major car companies to look for ways to use their resources more effectively. One way was to 'spread the risks' involved in research and development and in making cars in general. They also wanted to gain access to new markets. Austin Rover decided that the best way to achieve this was through **collaboration** with another car firm and in 1979 the company signed an agreement with Honda. They chose Honda for a number of reasons:

■ Honda has an outstanding reputation for engineering – particularly for engine design.
■ The company has a reputation for quality and high productivity.
■ Its major markets are in Japan and the Far East.
■ It was a firm of a similar size to Austin Rover.

There would be no basis for a deal if Austin Rover had nothing to offer Honda, though. As it was the company could claim:

■ a reputation for innovative design
■ expertise in suspension systems
■ dedication to high technology
■ its major markets were in Europe.

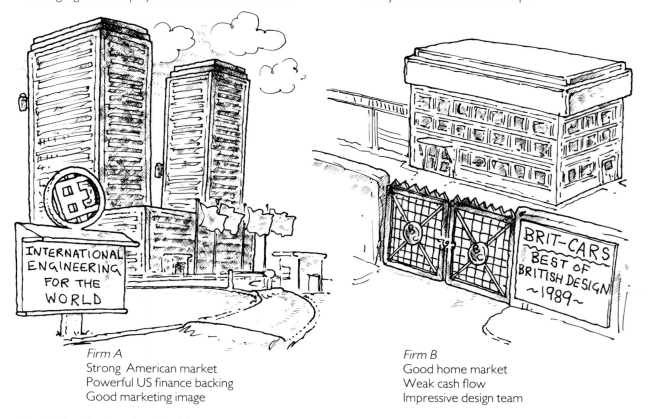

Firm A
Strong American market
Powerful US finance backing
Good marketing image

Firm B
Good home market
Weak cash flow
Impressive design team

Fig. 2.12   **The benefits of collaboration**

The first collaboration was on the Ballade, a car that Honda had developed but which Austin Rover adapted to produce its own version – the Triumph Acclaim – which was to cater for the 'lower medium sector of the market'. This model sold more than 130,000 models across Europe in four years. In 1981 the two firms agreed to manufacture a completely new car together – Project XX, a new Rover 800 executive saloon. As an Austin Rover spokesman said:

'It involved a remarkable degree of trust, for each company accepted the design responsibility for particular aspects of the vehicle. But perhaps more importantly, each relinquished responsibility for certain key areas to the other partner.

'At the same time each company retains its own manufacturing autonomy and product identity. So while the car, to be launched in the UK this year [1986] will have common components, the Austin Rover version will have a different exterior and interior style to the Honda version.'

EXERCISE

1 Explain how the rise in the price of oil in the 1970s badly affected car manufacturers.
2 Why did this lead them to consider 'joint ventures'? (Make sure that you explain clearly what a 'joint venture' is.)
3 How can you tell from the passage that one result of Austin Rover/Honda collaboration would be that both companies should each gain access to a new market?
4 Explain what you understand by the term 'medium lower section of the market'.
5 What was the first full joint venture between the two companies?
6 Why did Austin Rover say that this joint venture involved a 'remarkable degree of trust'?
7 In what way could the companies have been said to keep their own identity during the venture?

EXTENSION ACTIVITY

Research another example of a 'joint venture' – there may be one in your area. Try to find out the following:

(a) why the two firms decided to collaborate;
(b) what each could offer the other;
(c) how the customers benefit from this collaboration – if at all;
(d) the effect on the price and quality of the product;
(e) how successful the collaboration has been for the firms in terms of increased sales, reduced costs, higher profits, etc.;
(f) any problems that collaboration has produced.

Write a report on your findings.

2.10 From sole trader to private limited company

The sole trader

When Dai was a sole trader he alone was responsible for the running of the company; he could be taken to court if the law was broken either by himself or by anybody that he employed; he could distribute any profits that the company made, but he was also personally responsible for any losses that the company made. As you can see, being a sole trader does not prevent you from getting other people to work for you in the firm, but you 'carry the can' for anything that happens.

Some of the *advantages* of being a sole trader are:

- Independence and freedom of action – nobody to disagree with you.
- Satisfaction of 'doing it yourself'.
- You keep all the profits.
- It is an alternative to unemployment.

Some of the *disadvantages* are:

- Nobody to consult with.
- Lack of all-round specialism.
- Shortage of capital.
- Unlimited liability for all debts.
- Small, so unable to benefit from economies of scale, i.e. lower costs from being a large company (see Unit 6, Section 6.6).
- Lack of continuity – the business is dissolved on the death of the owner.

The partnership

When Dai and Elwyn formed a partnership they became *jointly* responsible for the running of the firm and any debts that it might have. They also received joint benefit of any profits earned – unless their partnership agreement stated otherwise.

Some of the *advantages* of forming a partnership are:

- Two, or more, people to discuss problems.
- More capital and specialist skills will be available.
- Risks will be shared.

Some of the *disadvantages* are:

- There is room for disagreement and it may be difficult to arrive at decisions.
- There may still be skill and capital shortages.
- At least one partner must retain limited liability.
- The partnership is dissolved if one of the partners leaves or dies – there is still no continuity.

The limited company

When Dai and Elwyn formed a private limited company they became incorporated so that the company and its members had a separate legal existence. This meant that:

- Limited liability could be offered to all members of the company and they could still play their part in the running of the business.
- A Board of Directors headed by the Chairman is set up.
- They can sell shares as long as they do not advertise them.
- The company can be sued in its own name.
- The company will continue even after the departure or death of one of its members.

A public limited company is similar except that it can advertise its shares and sell them on the Stock Exchange.

Incorporation obviously allows a company to grow; limited liability encourages people to invest and legal protection will encourage people to work for it. It does mean, however, that control of the company may well pass out of the hands of its founders, and not everybody may welcome that.

From sole trader to private limited company

Jim Smith was left £1,000 in a will by his aunt. He had always wanted to run his own company, so he used the money plus a bank loan to set it up. He became a **sole trader** and found that in many ways he liked it. In time, however, he decided that he wanted to take on a **partner**.

Business boomed and Jim was advised that **incorporation** held many advantages for him. He set up a **private limited company** and really thought that he had 'made it' in the financial world. Much to his disappointment, however, he found that the Stock Exchange was still closed to him.

He had a bit of a worry when a General Election was held and there was a rumour that one of the parties might **nationalise** his business; the other party promised to **privatise** it again should this be done, however.

Unfortunately there was a big slump in the market and Jim found it impossible to maintain his business, so he sought liquidation. His shareholders were very relieved that they had **limited liability**. His workers were unwilling to accept **redundancy** though, and decided to set up a **co-operative**. It survived for a year but was then forced out of business.

Fig. 2.13　The growth of business

QUESTIONS

1　Explain the meaning of the words in **bold**. (9)
2　What are the *two* aspects of being a sole trader that Jim might have liked? (2)
3　Why do you think that he might have decided 'in time' to take on a partner? (3)
4　Can you think of *one* problem that this might have caused? (1)
5　What are *three* of the advantages that incorporation would bring? (3)
6　What step would he have had to take to open the door of the Stock Exchange to his shares? Why do you think that this was impossible for him? (3)
7　Why were his shareholders so relieved that they had limited liability? (2)

8　Describe briefly the way in which you think that decisions may have been taken when the firm was a co-operative and explain how you think that this would differ from when Jim was running it. (6)
9　Why do you think that the co-operative eventually failed? (5)
10　Imagine that you are a politician. Write a short speech arguing: *either* that Jim's firm should be nationalised; *or* that, having been nationalised it should be privatised. Use as many of the general arguments as you can think of. (6)

(40)

3.1 Different roles within a business: a school

Let us start with an example with which you are familiar – a school. It may not strike you as a 'business' in the same way that a building works or chemical company does, but remember that it is an organisation that provides a **service** – as opposed to making a **product** – and that is your education. So it has to be organised to do this in the most efficient way possible.

Obviously all schools will vary in details of their organisation but the basic **structure** is likely to be similar in most cases. At the time of writing most schools are run by the **Local Education Authority**. This is part of the local council that is concerned with education. The **Chief Education Officer** oversees all schools in a particular area. The schools themselves are run by a **Board of Governors** which will have local councillors, parents, representatives from the teachers of the school and often a 'student governor' to represent the pupils. These will only meet a few times per term, however, so the school is run, on a day-to-day basis, by the **Headteacher** who is 'ultimately responsible' for anything that happens in the school. The

headteacher will usually have two or three **Deputy Headteachers**, at least one of whom takes charge of what is taught in the school – the **curriculum** – and another who looks after the welfare and discipline of the students – the **pastoral** aspect. One of these will also look after 'day-to-day' problems that arise in schools, such as organising 'cover' for absent teachers – the **administrative** side of it.

The next 'layer of management' is that of the **Faculty Heads** who directly organise a number of subjects (some schools do not have them), followed by **Heads of Department** who are responsible for different subjects within the school and the **Heads of Year/House** who look after the welfare of a section of students either of a particular year or a particular house, depending on how the school is organised. The Heads of Department will have **subject teachers** who answer to them, while the Heads of Year will control the activities of the **tutors**. Remember that most teachers will be both subject teachers and tutors, as will many Heads of Department.

Fig. 3.1

Each person who has some control over others is said to have a certain **span of control** which simply means the number of people for whom they are responsible. A small span of control enables you to know the others well and makes it easier to keep a watch on their activities. On the other hand, it can cause problems if there are 'personality clashes' between the people concerned. The opposite obviously applies for a large span of control. An **organisation tree** makes the **chain of command** very clear, i.e. who tells whom what to do.

EXERCISE

1 Explain the meaning of the following words:
   (a) responsible;
   (b) delegate;
   (c) span of control;
   (d) chain of command.
   Explain the importance of each within the organisation tree of any business.
2 Look at Fig. 3.2. If the Deputy Headteacher in charge of Curriculum wishes to pass a message to the Head of R.E., who would that message probably be passed through?
3 If a Blue House Tutor has a problem that the Head of Blue House cannot solve, who would they be expected to speak to next?
4 How big is the Head of Technical Subjects' span of control?
5 Draw up a list showing the advantages and disadvantages of a *large* span of control.
6 Draw an organisation tree for your own school, showing as much detail as you can find. You could work in pairs and prepare displays for the wall. Is there any way in which you think the organisation at your school can be improved? Perhaps you could write down your ideas on a piece of paper and make an appointment to discuss them with your headteacher.

EXTENSION ACTIVITY

Either visit, or write to, a business that is known to you. Ask about the different jobs that are done and 'who is in charge of whom'. Draw up its organisation tree from the information that you are given.

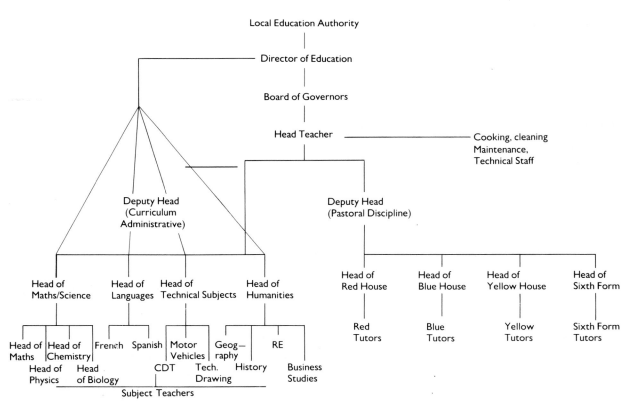

Fig. 3.2   A possible organisation tree for a secondary school

3.2 Different roles within a business: a manufacturing company

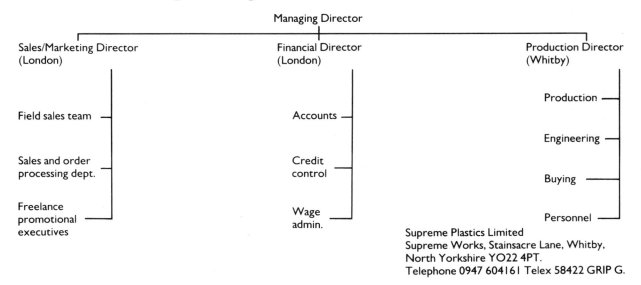

Fig. 3.3 Organisation tree for a manufacturing firm

Consider the organisation tree in Fig. 3.3. It belongs to a plastics company that has its administrative offices in London but actually produces its goods in Whitby, Yorkshire.

As you can see, it is run by a management team, headed by a **Managing Director** who is responsible for the company and all its employees. Three people are immediately responsible to the Managing Director:

- **Sales/Marketing Director**
  He is based in London and is responsible for the selling of the product and the marketing strategies involved in this.
- **Financial Director**
  He is also based in London and is responsible for all the money matters of the business.
- **Production Director**
  He is based in Whitby where the product is actually made and he runs the factory there.

Each of these directors is in turn responsible for the running of three departments. Under Sales and Marketing there is:

- *Field Sales Team*
  This is a group of employees who sell the product 'in the field', i.e. they actually go out and seek customers for the company.

- *Sales and Order Processing Department*
  This department is more 'office based' than the field sales team. The personnel carry out the necessary paperwork when sales are made and also when the company itself places orders for supplies with which to make the product.

- *Freelance Promotional Executives*
  They carry out promotional work to increase sales by bringing the product to the attention of as many people who are likely to buy it as possible.

Under the Financial Director there is:

- *Accounts*
  Accounts personnel keep the books of the company (we shall look at business accounts in Unit 5). Thus they will enter all transactions into the books, draw up a **profit and loss account** and a **balance sheet** for each financial year as well as possibly drawing up **cash-flow budgets** for certain periods of time to estimate the cash position of the company and predict if extra loans will be needed.

- *Credit Control*
  This department controls the credit offered to customers and chases **bad debts** (money owed to the company).

□ *Wage Administration*
This is where the payment of wages to all the employees in the business is organised.

Under the Production Director there is:

□ *Production Manager*
The production manager is in charge of the actual making of the product.

□ *Engineering Manager*
The engineering manager is responsible for ensuring that the machinery is in working order and that the best technical support is available for production.

□ *Buying Manager*
The buying manager supervises the purchase of all the supplies that are needed to run the factory.

Finally, there is:

□ *Personnel Manager*
The personnel manager looks after the welfare of all the employees in the business, deals with any personal problems that might affect the work situation and deals directly with trade unions (see Unit 4, Section 4.6).

FOR DISCUSSION

It is important to remember that any organisation can be run successfully only if the members see themselves as part of a **team**. In other words, different departments depend on each other in different ways – they are **interdependent**.

Use the information given above and hold a group discussion to decide how the following might depend on each other:

(a) Marketing and Production;
(b) Finance and Buying;
(c) Finance and Research;
(d) Marketing and Research.

(Unit 6, Section 6.5 on the **product life cycle** gives more information and a 'real-life' example of interdependence which may be of help.)

Fig. 3.4   The importance of operating as a team

3.3 How are decisions arrived at?

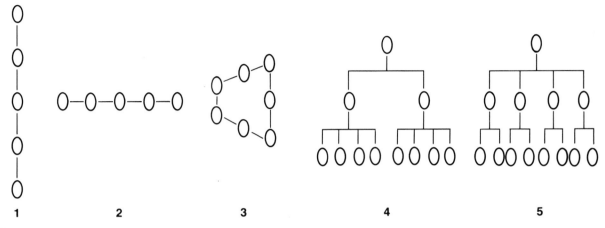

Fig. 3.5   Five organisation structures

We have already looked at organisation trees and the role that they play within businesses. There are other ways in which businesses can be organised and orders communicated, however.

Consider the following five organisation structures (shown in Fig. 3.5):

1   This could be said to be a very formal or **hierarchical** way of running a business. Each person takes orders from the person 'above' them and so there is absolutely no doubt about who you obey. It is also said to be a **vertical chain of command**. It has the obvious advantage of leaving everyone in no doubt about where they stand and reduces disputes about 'who does what'. So it could be said to be a very efficient system. On the other hand, it does not exactly make employees feel that they have an equal stake in the business and so may reduce their motivation to work for the company or make useful suggestions about its efficient running. In terms of 'who communicates with whom' it is inflexible; you only have access to your immediate 'superior' and 'subordinate'.

2   If the previous system was vertical this one is **horizontal**. Everyone is on an equal footing which removes some of the problems mentioned above, but communication is still restricted to two people which may make the spreading of information and the widespread discussion of ideas and problems difficult.

3   This is the most **democratic** form of organisation. Again, everyone is on an equal footing but communication is much more general; everyone has the chance to discuss issues together. If you think back to the idea of the

co-operative (Unit 2, Section 2.7), this is the form or organisation that you might expect there. It has the undoubted advantage of making everyone feel part of the business, which is likely to lead to a happier, better motivated workforce. On the other hand, it is not at all clear who makes the decisions and who has the final say in the event of disagreement. This system may work out satisfactorily when things are going well but does not necessarily lend itself to the easy resolution of problems.

4   At first glance, this and the following form of organisation look similar to the tree that we looked at in Section 3.1 and also to each other. Close examination will show that this is not the case. We have already looked at the concept of **span of control** – the number of people that one person has working directly under him or her. In this example, there are only two 'sub-managers' and each has several people under them.

5   In this structure, on the other hand, there are a number of 'sub-managers', each with just two people underneath them. It could be said that the work is more evenly 'spread' in this example than in the previous one while, on the other hand, the work is going to be more 'co-ordinated' in (4) because there are fewer people 'in control'.

All these are examples of **formal communication**. Under these systems you only 'formally communicate' with the person next in line.

Of course people in any organisation do not *just* talk to the person next in the chain of command! There will be a widespread network of **informal communication**. People will talk in the coffee bar, over lunch, over a drink in the evening; they will 'drop in' to each other's offices, they may play golf together. As much, if not more, may actually be decided in this way as through the 'formal channels of communication'.

EXERCISE

1 Explain in your own words the difference between **formal** and **informal** communication.
2 Draw up a table explaining the advantages and disadvantages of each of the different types of organisation structure.
3 Consider the following story:

Make-Anything Ltd were having 'motivation problems' with some of their staff. Joe Johnson was in charge of Accounts and he had three assistants under him: Tricia Jones, Fred Hill and Simon Gomez. Jean Rooksby in Personnel, on the other hand, had only one person to help – John Hargraves. For some reason – not related to the workload as far as anyone else could see – Ken Giles in Purchasing had five assistants: Una Horton, Yolande Rover, Jim Jones, Ron Tucker and Len Dodsworth. Rita Fairfax was the General Manager but the assistants, in particular, found it hard to see her and this 'alienated' them further from the company.

(a) Draw an organisation tree for the company – identify each member of the staff mentioned by his or her initials.
(b) Try to identify all the reasons why various employees feel dissatisfied.
(c) Explain how you might remedy the problems and draw up the 'alternative' organisation tree that you think would be an improvement.

3.4 Different types of production

Fig. 3.6 The beginnings of production

The heart of any manufacturing business is the **production department**. This is where the goods are actually made and it is their sale, and the revenue raised by this, that keeps the company in business and pays the wages of all the employees.

Many different types of people will be involved in production. The process will really start with **research and development**. This may well be a separate department and it is where the ideas about *what* can be produced and the best *way* of producing it will be found. The people employed at this end of the business will tend to be **scientists** – people with the ideas for new products and techniques of production.

The structure of different production departments will vary. Usually there will be a **Chief Engineer** who oversees the machinery used within the department and is responsible for ensuring that it is in good working order. Underneath the Chief Engineer there will be a number of other engineers who will carry out any necessary maintenance. In charge of the whole of production there

will be a **Production Manager** who is responsible for the whole of the output of the company. In direct contact with the 'shop floor' there will be **supervisors** or **foremen/ women** who oversee the **production workers** who actually make the product.

EXERCISE

As you have seen in Section 3.2 the Production Director is responsible for running the whole plant. Who would he or she consult if any of the following problems arose in the production area?

(a) Workers were taking an extra quarter-hour for their lunch-breaks.
(b) There were complaints from customers that the product did not work. (There may be more than one reason for this and this could produce more than one answer.)
(c) Production was being continually halted because of machine breakdowns.

Production itself may be of one of three types:

1 **Job production**

This is where production consists of 'one job at a time', i.e. items are made **individually**. As we saw when we looked at the Division of Labour (see Unit 1, Section 1.3) most factories are *not* organised like this now. The most common examples would be in places like craft shops where the whole appeal of the items is that it is 'hand made' and 'individual'. The reason why this form of production is not much used is that it does tend to be rather slow; it does have the advantage of producing more interesting goods, however, as well as giving greatly increased 'job satisfaction' to those involved.

2 **Batch production**

In this case goods are made 'in batches', i.e. in groups. Newspapers are produced like this. They come out each day and so there is a time deadline within which each 'batch' must be produced in order to be sent out to the different areas.

3 **Flow production**

Most modern production is organised according to this principle. Production is a 'continuous flow' off a production line. Everyone has an allotted job to do and production is continuous to meet steady demand.

(For a practical exercise on factory production, see 'The Hat Game' in Unit 10, Section 10.4.)

1.

2.

3.

Fig. 3.7   Different types of production

3.5 The Bertolini Brothers

The Bertolini brothers decide to set up a factory manufacturing exotic Italian food. There are two of them – Antonio and Mario – and they run the business alone.

In time, however, they find an increasing number of shops are prepared to sell their food. They decide to expand, and a number of their friends are prepared to put in money to help them – in return, of course, for a share of their profits.

The Bertolinis now have sufficient funds to take on some help, and all the members of their family are keen to join in. Frederico is very extrovert and loves travelling; Maria is notoriously careful with money; Cesare is very organised and is good at handling people, and Franco is an expert cook. Each has two assistants under him or her.

When they take on ten production workers difficulties start to arise because one of the workers is a union organiser and the Bertolinis don't think much of unions . . .

QUESTIONS

1 What form of business organisation would the Bertolinis be likely to opt for when starting their business? (2)

2 Name two possible sources of funds that they would be likely to have to start off the business – *apart from* a bank loan. (2)

3 If you were their bank manager, what sort of questions would you ask them before allowing them to take out a bank loan? (6)

4 Suggest some of the difficulties and problems that the Bertolinis may have found when they first started producing the food on their own. (4)

5 How is the injection of funds from friends who want a share of the profits likely to change the structure of the business? (1)

6 Using the clues in the text draw up an organisation tree for Bertolini Ltd after the entry of the rest of the family. Be careful to use the proper name for each job and link it with the relevant family member. (15)

(30)

4.1 Financial motivation

For simplicity the reasons why we work can be divided into just two categories: financial and non-financial.

Whatever other factors are involved, there can be no doubt that a very important reason for working is for money – we could not survive without it. Payment for a job can be one of two types:

- **Time rates**
  As the name suggests this involves payment for the period of time that you work – usually worked out on a rate per hour. So a firm may advertise for a cleaner to work for £2.50 per hour; a supply teacher in a school may be employed at £10 per hour.

- **Piece rates**
  This is payment 'by results' – in other words according to how much successful work you do. So a double-glazing salesman may be paid a certain amount per sale, a car worker a certain amount per car (or part of car) produced. There are obviously only a limited number of jobs where it is possible to operate this system; for example, how do you measure the work of a nurse? Also, in most cases where it does apply, a fairly low 'basic wage' is offered and all extra is 'bonus'.

Fig. 4.1   Reasons for working

FOR DISCUSSION

The following list includes some of the advantages of both systems of pay. Read through it and pick out the advantages of: (a) time rates, and (b) piece rates:

Encourages hard work.
Needs little supervision.
Allows people to plan their spending.
Pays people 'what they are worth'.
Ensures that all people receive a decent wage.
One person's pay is not affected by the actions of others.
The pay received does not depend on luck.
Can be applied to all occupations.
Is easy to calculate.
Does not encourage a rushed or shoddy job.
Rewards extra effort and penalises laziness.

Pool your findings as a class and discuss which system *you* think to be preferable and your reasons for your choice.

Look at the wage slip in Fig. 4.2. There are a number of things that you need to note:

The **total pay** is the total amount that the worker earns – the rate per hour multiplied by the number of hours worked. That is not the same as the amount of money the worker takes home, however – the **take home pay** or the **net pay**. The difference between the two is accounted for by deductions of various types:

1 **Income Tax (PAYE)**
This is money that is taken by the government in order to pay for services that we all use – hospitals and medical care, education, roads, housing, defence – known as **public goods**. PAYE stands for Pay As You Earn. This applies in most jobs and the money is automatically deducted from your pay before you receive it. Where people are 'self-employed', however, they are often not covered by PAYE and they will receive an annual tax bill.

2 **National Insurance**
This is also money that is taken by the government – specifically by the Department of Health and Social Security. It goes towards the state pension when you retire, unemployment pay if you should lose your job, and sick pay should you become ill.

3 **Superannuation**
Many jobs have their own pension scheme to supplement that of the state. This is also deducted in the form of regular contributions.

4 **Trade Union Subscription**
This is a contribution towards a body that will negotiate your wages, look after your conditions of employment, represent you in any dispute with your employer and insure you against any problems at work. Many unions offer other 'fringe benefits', such as social facilities and holiday rest homes.

PAY ADVICE FOR							
					ENDING 02/12/1988		C.C.770

		PAYMENTS UNITS	VALUE	ITEM	DEDUCTIONS VALUE	BALANCE	
ITEM	T/N						
BASIC	T	4000	125.00	TAX	28.00		
O/T 1.5	T	800	27.50	NAT. INS	14.62		
				SUPERAN	0.00		
				TU SUBSC	3.25		

TAX PERIOD 35
TAX CODE 260L
NI No
BANK CODE NM6 386 5 8D
BANK A/C

HOL. BAL. 1
HOL. BAL. 2
HOL. BAL. 3

GROSS TO DATE 987.13
TAX TO DATE 171.00
PENS TO DATE
NI TO DATE 88.89

PAYROLL EMP. REF.
003402900
TAXABLE PAY
162.50
NON-TAXABLE PAY
0.00
TOTAL PAY
162.50
TOTAL DEDUCTIONS
45.87
NET PAY
116.63
ROUNDING
B/FWD. 0.00 C/FWD. 0.00
METHOD OF PAYMENT
CASH

UNIPAY SYSTEMS (C)

Fig. 4.2

4.2 Non-financial motivation

Very few people could be happy in a job *just* because of the money, however. There must be other things to **motivate** us, i.e. to encourage us to enjoy a job and do it to the best of our ability. Imagine that you are in a well-paid job where working conditions were cold, damp and dirty; where the people that you worked with were unfriendly; where there was no recognition given of your talents, no praise or encouragement; where there was no prospect of promotion or betterment and no prospect of fulfilling yourself 'as a person'. How does this prospect appeal to you?

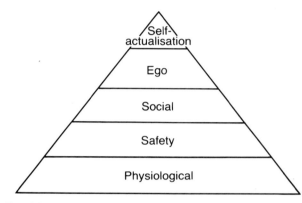

Fig. 4.3 Maslow's hierarchy of needs

Look at the diagram in Fig. 4.3. This is known as **Maslow's Hierarchy of Needs**. Abraham Maslow was a psychologist who tried to work out what people needed to satisfy themselves and to be happy. This was important both for the people themselves and also to help industry produce conditions in which its workers were 'well-motivated'. The important thing to remember about this is the word 'hierarchy'; this means that one need stands on top of another and that the 'higher' needs cannot be satisfied until the 'lower' needs have been met. This will become clearer as we look at each layer in more detail.

- **Physiological**
  Physiology is the science of the human body and so these can be described as 'bodily needs' – the need to eat, drink and maintain a tolerable level of comfort. If we are hungry, thirsty or uncomfortable we are not in a position to appreciate much else.
- **Safety**
  We all need to feel that we are not in danger in a job (apart from people who spend some time taking part in dangerous sports or those who deliberately choose a job with an element of risk). Working conditions must reflect this.
- **Social**
  Human beings are, on the whole, outward-going, 'gregarious' creatures who need conversation and contact with others. Employers who take this into account tend to have a happier workforce.
- **Ego**
  Even the most modest people have an 'ego' – a sense of themselves and of their achievements. There are two types of ego that must be taken into account;
  (a) Personal – we must be given a sense of our own achievements;
  (b) Inter-personal – we must feel that others are aware of them also.
- **Self-actualisation**
  This is the vaguest and most difficult to define and understand – and yet it is also the most important. It is the 'icing on the cake' that relatively few people achieve. It means that you achieve everything that you expect of yourself in a way that completely satisfies you – or as nearly as possible because everyone has some regrets. It may not be at work but in some other activity, for example catching the largest salmon ever or achieving a world record at swimming. How many of us can hope to achieve these? Of course some people would not aspire to anything like that and may be completely satisfied with a happy home life and contentment at work. As you can see, the prospect for employers being able to help in this is very limited.

EXERCISE

Copy out the five headings of Maslow's Hierarchy and read through the following actions that an employer might take. Place each under the heading which you think that it will satisfy:

Building a social club.
Designing a promotion structure that everyone feels that they have a chance to climb.
Increasing wages.
Organising a works dance.
Offering a bonus for better work performance.
Checking conditions of work regularly.
Ensuring that good work is always recognised and praised.
Building a subsidised works canteen.
Having only one canteen in which everybody eats – from the Managing Director to the apprentice.
Giving employees a chance to discuss their jobs and careers and offering them advice about the best moves for them.
Appointing a Health and Safety Officer.

Pick out five which you think are the most important and should be done first, putting them in order. Which is the most common need that is being satisfied by your choice?

EXTENSION ACTIVITY

John, the Personnel Manager, receives the following memorandum from Ken, the Managing Director:

TO: John Sinclair   REF: KB/MP
FROM: Ken Brown   DATE: 10.10.88

John, I am worried. Morale among the workers seems to be very low at the moment. This is showing itself in a number of ways, some small and some not so small. For instance I was walking through the works the other day and a number of the workers were not actually doing anything; those that were did not appear to be exerting themselves, and they know as well as I do that we only have a couple of weeks to finish the project to meet the deadline for the contract and that if we manage it there will be a very hefty bonus for them. More than that, I am used to exchanging greetings with them when I walk through yet not one of them even looked up. I have got the shop steward on my back for the smallest things – only the other day, as you know, she threatened to call the whole works out simply because of a leaking ceiling in one of the machine rooms. Hardly worth a strike, is it? They are also calling for a new canteen for everybody. They have got one for themselves at the moment so I cannot see their point – can you? She also said something about management never talking to the workers; well, what is there to talk about, for goodness' sake? They get good wages – what more do they want? I would welcome any thoughts that you have on the matter because I am worried that we will miss the deadline for the contract if motivation and effort does not improve. You have just been on this 'staff relations training course'; what have you learned?

Your task: As the Personnel Manager write him a memorandum about what you have learned. Explain carefully any recommendations that you make and pick out points from the passage that indicate to you that Ken's attitude is making matters worse. Explain why and how he could remedy matters.

4.3 Skills and aptitudes

A **skill** is something that you are able to do; an **aptitude** is something that you have a natural talent for and can do without much effort.

EXERCISE

Consider the following aptitudes:

good head for figures
pleasant manner with people
physical strength
dexterity
technical ability
good with hands
good at problem solving

Try to match them up with the correct jobs out of the following list (some may need more than one):

electrician
dustman
salesperson
engineer
accountant
seamstress
carpenter
computer programmer

When you are choosing the sort of occupation that you wish to take up it is important that you are aware of your own strengths and weaknesses so that you look in areas where you have some natural ability. A firm will also try to assess the aptitudes of candidates for jobs to try to pick out those who will be most suited. There are a number of ways of doing this, and many companies use them all.

The testimonial

This is a general 'report' on you as a person and as a worker from a previous employer, or from your school if you have just left and are applying for your first job. Apart from your application form this will be the first thing that a firm sees about you; the testimonial may be used to decide who to interview when there are a number of candidates for the one job.

The reference

You may be asked to give the names of two people who will give you a reference. One of these will probably be your current employer so it is unusual for a firm to take up references until after an interview when they are almost sure they will want to employ you. A reference is a confidential report and will answer specific questions such as: did you co-operate with colleagues? Were you punctual? . . . and so on.

Fig. 4.4   Jobs vacant

The interview

A 'short-list' will be drawn up from all those applying and they will be called to an interview which is really a conversation during which the firm finds out more about you – and you about them!

Consider the following interview in which Mr Detray, the Personnel Manager for Make-a-lot Engineering Products, is interviewing Rod, a school leaver, for a job as a trainee engineer.

Mr D: Good morning. My name is Stephen Detray. I am the Personnel Manager here and I will be interviewing you for the vacancy for the trainee engineer.
Rod: Hi.
Mr D: Er, quite. Well, what can you tell me about yourself?
Rod: Not a lot, really. I've just left school, I was looking for a job and my mate told me to apply here.
Mr D: Really. Apart from study for your exams what else did you do at school?
Rod: Nothing. I hated the place.
Mr D: Nevertheless, you will expect to get a few GCSEs when the results come out?
Rod: I very much doubt it. I skipped school whenever I could.
Mr D: I imagine that you must have been quite good at Maths if you think that you would be able to train as an engineer.
Rod: That was my worst subject of the lot.
Mr D: Why did you apply for this job, then?
Rod: Like I told you, my mate suggested it. I didn't know you needed to be good at Maths, did I?
Mr D: What do you do in your spare time, any hobbies?
Rod: Well, I go down the boozer on Friday night and, er . . .
Mr D: Thank you very much. We will be in touch.
Rod: Cheerio.

EXERCISE

Read through the interview between Mr Detray and Rod. Do you think that Mr Detray will be in touch? Pick out all the points in the interview where Rod 'went wrong'. Re-write the dialogue, with Mr Detray asking the same questions but with Rod giving the sort of answers that might help him get the job.

Points to look out for in an interview

- Dress smartly. It might only be 'an appearance' but appearances can count in these situations.
- Be polite. There is no need to speak in a very formal way but don't talk to the interviewer in a sloppy, lazy way.
- Make sure that you know a little about the job and what skills or aptitudes *you* would need to be able to do it *before* you go to the interview, so that you appear to have taken an interest and are not just wasting the interviewer's time.
- **Be positive about yourself**. Look for your own good points and ensure that you put them over. You do not want to appear a braggart (it is often good to show that you are aware of your weaknesses also), but if you do not sell yourself nobody will do it for you.
- The employer is likely to want to know a little about you as a 'whole person', so stress your full range of interests.

Aptitude tests

As well as the interview, many firms will set tests to see if people are suited to a job. Jobs in computing and information technology are usually allocated in this way, as are many jobs which involve the use of numerical or technical skills. These tests are believed to indicate whether people could actually *do* a particular job.

EXERCISE

1 Divide into pairs, think of a job description and interview each other for it; alternatively, your teacher might want to do the interviewing. This will be good practice for when you do it 'for real'.
2 Write your own reference! Exchange with your partner and see if you each agree with the other's assessment. Can you think of other skills or aptitudes your partner may have that are not mentioned? Are there any skills mentioned that you didn't know the other possessed?

4.4 Qualifications

As we have just seen (in Section 4.3) it is important to have an aptitude for a particular job, as well as being able to present yourself well at an interview. This is not always enough, however, and it may be necessary to have certain **qualifications**. They can include one or more of the following:

- **GCSE**
  These are examinations in a number of subjects that you will take at the end of your fifth year at school. It may qualify you for unskilled jobs and those which demand a 'low-level entry qualification' but which offer 'on the job training'.
- **A-Level**
  Some people stay at school to study to a higher level than GCSE. They can study 2–4 subjects to Advanced Level in the sixth form, usually for two years. This provides either a qualification to enter a degree course at university or enables you to enter jobs around the 'trainee management' level. At the time of writing an 'A–S Level' is in the final stages of preparation. This is half-way towards an A-Level and aims at a wider range of student.
- **CPVE**
  The initials stand for Certificate of Pre-Vocational Education. It is also run in the sixth form and is a one-year course that specifically trains young people to enter the job market. To that end it involves a considerable amount of 'work experience' to accustom students to the work situation and gives them experience that they can offer to employers.
- **TVEI**
  The Technical, Vocational, Educational Initiative is part of increasing numbers of GCSE courses – as well as entering some sixth forms. It is run by the Manpower Services Commission and it aims to increase 'skills based education' in areas of expanding employment such as Information Technology (see Unit 9).
- **BTEC National**
  This is also a 'vocational' course, but one that includes quite a high degree of academic learning. It is run at sixth form, tertiary and other colleges of further education.
- **BTEC Higher**
  The Higher National Diploma and Certificate are courses that are run at colleges of further and higher education. They can be studied either on a full-time basis, or part-time while you are working. They offer a qualification in a vocational subject which is a bit lower than a university degree. They are often a necessary step to promotion in such areas as Engineering, Accountancy and Law.
- **University Degree**
  These are three- (or occasionally four-) year courses of advanced academic study that enable the holder to enter a number of types of 'white collar' jobs. Possessors of a good degree can go on to take a Master's degree and a Doctorate – which is really the furthest that you can go in a particular subject.
- **Postgraduate training**
  Some jobs require specific training after the degree is completed. Teachers have to complete a Postgraduate Certificate in Education (PGCE) which involves some 'educational theory' and some teaching practice. Social workers have to complete a Certificate of Qualification for Social Work CQSW which similarly involves some college work and some practical social work.
- **Apprenticeship**
  Some jobs train through work. This tends to apply to 'skilled manual' jobs – engineering workers, electricians, carpenters, hairdressers, plumbers, joiners, bricklayers, etc. It will usually take five years before you are assumed to be fully competent at the job. During this time you will probably go to college on day release and will receive a lower rate of pay than the full 'adult' wage.

Fig. 4.5   At the job centre

There are also a number of government training schemes to help those who find it difficult to get a job – mainly aimed at young people:

- **Youth Training Scheme**
  The Youth Training Scheme (YTS) is now a two-year course during which a firm receives a grant from the government training agency to train a youngster. All 16–18 year olds will participate if they cannot find other

employment and, at the time of writing, the government is considering stopping unemployment benefit to those who refuse to participate. It gives work experience in an organisation, necessary skills, at least thirteen weeks off-the-job training in social, life and work-related skills and a trainee allowance.

■ Job Start

To try to encourage young people to accept jobs that pay low wages, rather than remain unemployed, the government adds an amount of money to the weekly wage of those earning less than a minimum amount in a job after having been out of work for over a year.

EXERCISE

1 Choose eight jobs of different types and research the exact entry qualifications needed and training offered. The school Careers Officer, and careers room, the Head of Sixth Form (if you have one) and the library all might have useful information. Write up your findings in the form of a report.

2 The table in Fig. 4.6 shows the number of people covered by the different employment and training measures brought in by the Government between 1983 and 1988. Look at it carefully and write out the schemes in order of rate of growth. Which has grown most quickly? Which have disappeared altogether?

EXTENSION ACTIVITY

Research into all the new job and training schemes that are available now for the unemployed – particularly the young. The town library and advice centre (i.e. Citizens Advice Bureau) will be able to help. What facilities are available in *your* area for training the unemployed – and for what? Again write up your findings in the form of a report and comment yourself on whether you think that these offer acceptable solutions for the problems of unemployment. Add any alternative ideas you may think of.

Fig. 4.6   Numbers covered by special employment and training measures

Great Britain, thousands

	August 1983	August 1984	August 1985	August 1986	March 1987	March 1988
Enterprise Allowance	6	39	49	64	80	94
Community Programme	83	123	146	230	255	255
Job Release Scheme	83	89	57	33	27	27
Young Workers Scheme	95	65	45	14	0	0
New Workers Scheme	0	0	0	11	63	767
Youth Training Scheme	101	330	328	330	400	600
Youth Opportunities	108	0	0	0	0	0
Temporary Short-term Working	42	12	0	0	0	0
Total	518	658	625	682	825	1,052

4.5 Equal opportunities at work

One regulation that affects businesses relates to **discrimination** on the grounds of sex. Employers are not allowed to pay different wages or refuse somebody a job simply because the employee is a man or a woman. There are two main pieces of government legislation that relate to this:

1 **The Equal Pay Act (1970)**
   This states that women are entitled to equal pay with men when they are doing work that is 'the same or broadly similar'. In other words it is illegal to pay a male and female clerk who have similar duties – filing, looking after the accounts of the office, etc. – a different wage when they are doing similar work.
      This Act was **amended** – changed slightly – in 1984 to read that men and women should be paid equally for work 'of equal value'. So the clerks may have different duties but if those duties have the same value to the firm they must be paid the same wage.

2 **The Sex Discrimination Act (1975)**
   This extended the above Act which just dealt with pay. It now became 'unlawful to treat anyone, on the grounds of sex, less favourably than a person of the opposite sex is or would be treated in the same circumstances'. It states that sex discrimination is not allowed in 'employment, education, the provision of housing, goods, facilities and services and advertising'. It is also unlawful to discriminate in employment because a person is married. The **Equal Opportunities Commission** was set up to try to enforce these Acts. It can carry out investigations where it suspects discrimination and, if this is confirmed, the commission can put out a notice ordering that it cease. It also helps people prepare cases for tribunals and educates people about their rights.

Obviously there are some jobs that do require a person of a certain sex; for example, it would not be reasonable for a female actress to claim discrimination if she were not given the part of Hamlet! This is known as **genuine occupational qualification (GOQ)** and allows exceptions to the Sex Discrimination Act.

The case of Miller v. Strathclyde District Council

A good example of the Sex Discrimination Act at work occurred in Scotland in 1985. A female PE teacher in Ayr applied for a job as Principal Teacher of PE at a school. In the Ayr district there were 30 Principal Teachers of PE, none of whom was female. On the other hand there were 14 Assistant Principals of PE, practically all of whom were female. In the previous ten years the 'complainant' (the person bringing the case) had applied for seven similar jobs without success. She was highly regarded by the

Fig. 4.7   Bricklayers

Headteacher at her school, but when she applied for the last job the male teacher in her department who also applied was called to interview, but neither she nor her female colleague was. Her Headteacher commented: 'You know that I am delighted with your work in every way. You must remember that it is a man who is leaving Grange Academy and it will be a man who will replace him. After all, it is the last bastion of male supremacy and they won't give up that easily.' The case was brought to an Industrial Tribunal, with the help of the Equal Opportunities Commission and the Tribunal 'had no hesitation in holding that the reasons why the complainant was not put on the short-list at Grange Academy was because of her sex'. It was not able, of course, to order the Education Authority to employ her as a Principal Teacher, but it awarded her **financial compensation** for injured feelings and the money that she would have lost for the next two years as a result of not being appointed to the post.

EXERCISE

Read through the example given of discrimination at work and answer the following questions.
1 Do you think that it was a coincidence that there were no female Principal Teachers in the Ayr district? Explain your answer.
2 Explain the statement, 'it is the last bastion of male supremacy'. Is that a good enough reason for not offering somebody a job?
3 What other information would *you* ask for if you were sitting in judgement on this case? What witnesses would you call? Write down the questions that you might ask *two* of them and the answers that they might give.

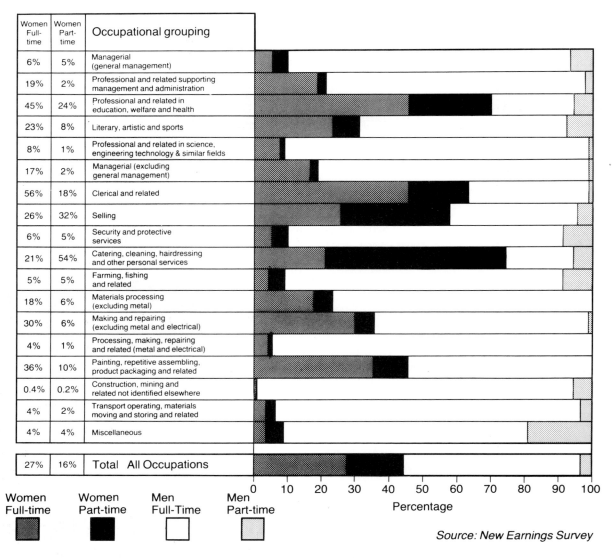

Women Full-time	Women Part-time	Occupational grouping
6%	5%	Managerial (general management)
19%	2%	Professional and related supporting management and administration
45%	24%	Professional and related in education, welfare and health
23%	8%	Literary, artistic and sports
8%	1%	Professional and related in science, engineering technology & similar fields
17%	2%	Managerial (excluding general management)
56%	18%	Clerical and related
26%	32%	Selling
6%	5%	Security and protective services
21%	54%	Catering, cleaning, hairdressing and other personal services
5%	5%	Farming, fishing and related
18%	6%	Materials processing (excluding metal)
30%	6%	Making and repairing (excluding metal and electrical)
4%	1%	Processing, making, repairing and related (metal and electrical)
36%	10%	Painting, repetitive assembling, product packaging and related
0.4%	0.2%	Construction, mining and related not identified elsewhere
4%	2%	Transport operating, materials moving and storing and related
4%	4%	Miscellaneous
27%	16%	Total All Occupations

Women Full-time ■ Women Part-time ■ Men Full-Time □ Men Part-time ▨

Percentage

Source: New Earnings Survey

Fig. 4.8   Percentage distribution of persons in employment by occupational grouping and sex, 1987

EXTENSION ACTIVITY

1 Study the table in Fig. 4.8 and pick out the *three* most popular occupations for women and the three most unpopular. Write a short paragraph by each occupation, explaining why this might be the case. Present the information given in the form of a **bar graph**.

2 Do you believe that the opportunity shown in figure 4.9 is really open to both male and female candidates?

3 Pick out all the indications from the advertisement in Fig. 4.10 of an 'intention to discriminate' both in the words and in the picture.

4 The advertisement shown in Fig. 4.11 won the approval of the Equal Opportunities Commission. Pick out all the reasons why.

5 Finally try to think of *five* jobs that might be said to have GOQ (look back to the previous page if you can't remember what that means). Bear in mind that 'a GOQ cannot be claimed for a job on the grounds that it requires physical strength or stamina'.

Do your friends think you're Superman?

If they do, test their opinion in an interview with us – convince our Sales Director that your friends are right, and you'll join a company that really is going places in the field of double glazing.

We can't guarantee a Lois Lane or Wonderwoman to hold your hand – but we can offer you super sales leads simply asking for conversion. And more expansion is planned in the very near future.

Write, giving full details of your experience, to:
John Summers,
Winterwarmth Double Glazing Ltd.,
Castle Road, Wellingborough.

Fig. 4.10

SALESMEN

Join the best metal-finishing company in Britain – if you can measure up to the demands of our tough sales operation. Earnings are entirely up to you. You'll have a very large sales territory and be backed by an HQ team that will support you through thick and thin provided you keep coming up with the goods!

There's a car with the job of course and a generous expense allowance to top a first-class basic salary and good commission rates. Write, giving details of your qualifications, experience and ambitions, to: J. G. Bowler, Sales Director, Metallic Products Limited, Caernarvon Road Industrial Estate, Kidderminster KA2 4RL.

Metallic Products
PUTTING INDUSTRY ON ITS METAL

This opportunity is open to both male and female candidates

Fig. 4.9

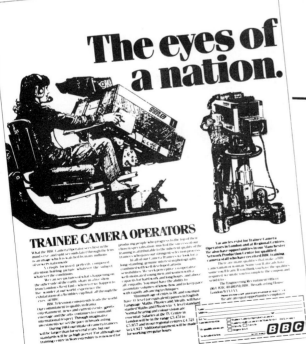

The eyes of a nation.

TRAINEE CAMERA OPERATORS

Fig. 4.11

4.6 Trade unions

When you are at work you may feel that you are not receiving sufficient wages for the job you are doing; similarly you might think that the conditions in which you are being asked to work are unacceptable, or you may have some other complaint.

You could storm into the manager's office and demand changes – the chances are that you would not get very far! That is why workers join together to form **trade unions** to negotiate on behalf of them all. The greater the proportion of the workforce that are members and the more willing they are to follow the decisions of the majority, the more likely it is that the management will take notice. If there is an agreement whereby all the workers in a firm have to join a union there is said to be a **closed shop.**

Trade unions can be divided into four categories:

1 **General unions**
Anybody can join these and their members are usually unskilled or semi-skilled workers. An example is the Transport and General Workers Union (TGWU).

2 **Craft unions**
People with particular skills join craft unions. As an example, skilled engineering workers tend to be members of the Amalgamated Union of Engineering Workers (AUEW).

3 **Industrial unions**
This is where one union acts for all the workers in one particular industry. These are far more common in Europe than in this country. The nearest example here is probably the National Union of Mineworkers (NUM), although a rival union grew up after the 1984 strike – the Union of Democratic Mineworkers (UDM) – and there is also a union for the 'pit deputies', the National Association of Colliery Overmen, Deputies and Shotfirers (NACODS).

4 **White-collar unions**
These are for non-manual workers such as the Manufacturing, Science and Finance Union (MSF), or the union for local government workers, the National and Local Government Officers' Association (NALGO).

Fig. 4.12   Different occupations

How are unions organised?

In the workplace a **shop steward** will be elected to represent the immediate grievances of workers to management. He or she will be one of the workers and will do his or her regular job on top of any trade-union responsibilities. If a dispute becomes serious, then **local officials** who are employed full time by the union to represent them in an area will become involved. If the dispute involves workers throughout the country it will be run by **national officials** led by the **General Secretary** who is usually elected by the whole membership.

How are unions brought together?

Trade unions have always felt the need to work together on a national basis in order to extend their influence. Thus most of them (88 at the time of writing) are affiliated to the **Trades Union Congress (TUC).** The TUC has a General Secretary and a full-time staff. Their policy is determined at their **Annual Congress,** to which all affiliated unions can send delegates and from which the **General Council** is elected to carry out the decisions of Congress and run the TUC throughout the year. The TUC has a particularly important role in resolving disputes between different unions and was very active in resolving the disagreements between the National Graphical Association (NGA) and the Society of Graphical and Allied Trades (SOGAT 82) on one hand and the Electrical, Electronic, Telecommunication and Plumbing Union (EETPU) on the other in the Wapping newspaper dispute (see Section 4.8).

What is the response of the employers?

As we have seen, trade unions have the job of winning the best possible wages and conditions for workers. Employers, on the other hand, have slightly different responsibilities. They need to run their business as efficiently as possible. This means trying to keep their costs down so that:

- There is money left for **profits** to reward people who have put their funds into the company and to encourage them to continue doing so.
- There is money left for new **investment** in the latest plant and machinery so that the goods can be produced more efficiently.
- They can keep their **prices** as low as possible so that they can sell as many goods as possible.

If a firm is not able to achieve these aims it may not be able to continue in business and all working in it may lose their jobs. A high wage increase may work against this and so there will be **bargaining** between the two sides. Some of the conditions that may be attached to a wage increase could include:

- Workers agreeing to produce more per person – higher **productivity.** This could be through greater effort, longer working hours or shorter breaks.
- Fewer people working in the workplace to keep the wage bill down. This might involve **compulsory redundancy** where people are forced to give up their job or **voluntary redundancy** where people are tempted to volunteer by the offer of large 'redundancy payments'. There could be **natural wastage** where people who retire are not replaced or an agreement to take on **fewer trainees.** As long as the remaining people work harder this should also lead to higher productivity.

Not surprisingly, unions are not usually keen to agree to conditions that will lead to redundancies.

Given the high degree of organisation of the unions, the employers have also felt the need to get together – albeit on a rather looser basis than the unions. They have a body called the **Confederation of British Industry (CBI),** which also holds annual conferences and provides advice and help for its members.

4.7 The negotiations game

Unions negotiate with management over a wide range of issues. The most obvious is **wages** – everybody would like their union to win for them the highest rate possible for the job. **Working conditions** are also very important – no one wishes to work in an unpleasant or unsafe environment. The fight against **compulsory redundancy**, whereby people are forced to leave their jobs, will be taken up by the union; in fact the union will represent the worker in almost any dispute with the management, whether large or small.

How are negotiations conducted?

Unions spend a lot of their time discussing wages. This is known as **collective bargaining**. For example, the union will put in an annual wage claim – say for 15 per cent. Management will put up its hands in horror and say that they cannot possibly afford so much – they can, at a pinch, just about manage 5 per cent. The unions declare that this is quite unacceptable – the lowest they could possibly sell to their members is 12 per cent. Management say that this is still out of the question, but if the workers can bring themselves to increase productivity they could offer 8 per cent.

So they settle – at 10 per cent!

What if it goes wrong?

Of course, the above example is highly simplified. In practice agreement is unlikely to be so easy; indeed, negotiations may break down. If that happens there are two courses of action that may be followed:

1 Appeal to arbitration
There is a body called the **Advisory Conciliation and Arbitration Service (ACAS)**. This is a committee made up of a group of 'independent' people – neither management nor trade unions. It is sometimes asked to look into a dispute that has reached deadlock and produce a recommendation. No one is legally forced to accept its findings, although there is great 'moral' pressure to do so.

2 Industrial action
If all else fails, workers may attempt to disrupt production in some way. This may take a number of forms:
   (a) **Go slow** – workers work as slowly as possible;
   (b) **Work to rule** – workers work just 'by the rule book' and do nothing extra);
   (c) **Overtime ban** – all workers work their basic hours – and no more.

All these will cause inconvenience to the firm without shutting it down completely. Customers and suppliers may hardly notice. The big advantage for the workers of any of

WE WANT 15% AND NOT A PENNY LESS

IMPOSSIBLE QUITE IMPOSSIBLE IT WOULD BANKRUPT ME!!!

MANAGER

12% IS THE VERY LEAST THE LADS AND LASSIES WILL ACCEPT

8% IS JUST POSSIBLE IF YOU WORK HARDER

..MUCH DISCUSSION FOLLOWED....

IT'S A DEAL 10%

Fig. 4.13 Wage negotiation

Fig. 4.14　Picket line during a strike

these forms of action is that management cannot deduct anything from their basic wages.

(d) **Strike** – this involves stopping work completely. A strike may be **official** – backed by the trade union nationally, or **unofficial** if it is without that backing. If it is official the trade union will usually try to make up at least some of the lost wages with strike pay. A strike is likely to lead to success only if everybody joins in – so a **picket line** will be formed outside the place of work to discourage people from entering and to prevent goods from leaving. Those who break the picket line are often known as **blacklegs** or **scabs**. The union will also try to persuade other workers not to handle – or to **black** – any goods that the company might manage to produce.

EXERCISE

1　Discuss as a class and make notes on the likely effects of a strike on:
(a) the firm;
(b) the workers;
(c) the suppliers.
What factors are likely to determine whether or not the strike is successful?

2　This is an exercise in 'Negotiation in Action'. Divide into equal groups of three or four students. Half the groups represent management, the others the union. You all work for the Wearland Doll Factory.

The background is as follows:

The firm employs 500 people making large dolls. At present the workers earn an average of £80 per week. This is well below the national average of £120 per week. In addition, prices rose by 5 per cent in the last year. The company has just released its accounts for the last year which reveal a post-tax profit of £1 million. This profit has been earned from a revenue of £5 million (1 million dolls sold at £5 each). From this you can work out the current wage bill and other costs. The firm has £2 million in its reserve fund but it does not wish to dip into it. A large competitor has recently reduced its operations but the market itself is shrinking and the firm's market researchers expect to sell only 800,000 dolls next year – unless up to £250,000 is spent on additional advertising. The firm would like a profit of at least £800,000 next year to meet its obligations to its shareholders and to finance investment. The employers may be prepared to concede extra money for a 'productivity' agreement that could involve redundancies. In any case they will only be convinced by hard figures and a well-presented case.

Your task:　Negotiate a mutually acceptable settlement, taking into account all the factors that have been mentioned. Each group could present its case to the class who could then 'discuss' their way to a settlement.

4.8 The changing role of the unions

As already indicated, unions have traditionally seen their main functions as fighting for higher wages and better working conditions. During the 1970s there was a series of big national strikes over pay. Arguably two of them – the Miners' Strike in 1974 and the Public Sector workers' strike in 1979 – influenced the fall of the government of the day. The rise in unemployment from 1.3 million in 1979 to 3.3 million in 1987 changed all that. It weakened the ability of the unions to ask for wage increases and concentrated their minds on the saving of jobs. In 1984–5 the miners struck again – but this time it was to oppose redundancies rather than to demand an increase in wages. The national newspaper dispute in Wapping occurred for similar reasons.

The Wapping Dispute

This would be an excellent subject for a project because it brings out a number of features that you have been studying – the function of trade unions, the impact of new technology on an industry and disputes *between* different unions.

Briefly the story is as follows: News International is a huge company that publishes newspapers and magazines and owns television and film companies. Its chairman is Rupert Murdoch. In 1985 he moved his printing works from London's Fleet Street, where national newspapers have traditionally been published, to Wapping in the East End of London, where new development is bringing the old dockland areas back to life. He introduced the latest technology for the printing of newspapers and magazines which, of course, needed fewer people to work it. For instance, the number of workers needed to produce the four titles in the group has fallen from 2,000 to 520 and the number needed to pack the papers has fallen from 1,800 to just 132.

The unions involved, principally the National Graphical Association (NGA) which represents the printers, and SOGAT '82 which represents the rest of the newspaper workers, claimed that the move was introduced to reduce jobs and push the unions out. Furthermore they claimed that they had not been properly consulted.

Murdoch, on the other hand, said that he was only introducing technology that all the other European countries already used and that it was opposition from the unions to such developments that had held Fleet Street back for so long.

The union members went on strike and Murdoch claimed that the 5,000 workers involved had 'dismissed themselves' by this action – so he sacked them! He found people to print his paper and journalists to work on it.

Fig. 4.15 Wapping dispute

Most controversially, from the point of view of the unions, was the fact that the electricians' union (EETPU) recruited workers from Southampton to install the machinery 'in secret' (according to the printing unions) and afterwards worked at the plant, consistently breaking the picket lines that the workers had set up.

Fig. 4.16

Murdoch made repeated offers of compensation to settle the dispute; at one stage he offered the unions his old printing press at Grey's Inn Road for a 'labour movement' newspaper. The unions insisted that the main issue was the reinstatement of the sacked workers and full union recognition at Wapping. Spirits flagged after more than a year of protesting outside the plant and the support that was hoped for from other unions never really materialised. So in February 1987 the dispute was called off. Rupert Murdoch is now firmly installed in Wapping producing national newspapers like *The Times, The Sunday Times*, the *Sun* and the *News of the World* and the sacked workers have not got their jobs back.

Fig. 4.17   Printers end of dispute

POINTS FOR DISCUSSION

1 In which 'category' of union do you think that the following belong:

   (a) the NGA;
   (b) SOGAT '82;
   (c) the EETPU?

How might this have influenced their behaviour?

2 Why do you think that Wapping seemed to be an attractive area for News International to move to?

3 Explain the phrase 'the latest technology . . . which, of course, needed fewer people to work it'.

4 Why do you think that Rupert Murdoch was so keen to introduce this technology?

5 Do you think that it made sense for the unions to call a strike? What other forms of action – if any – were open to them?

6 Was Murdoch justified in saying that the striking workers had 'dismissed themselves'?

7 Do you think that the behaviour of the workers in the EETPU was selfish or merely sensible?

8 As a union leader would *you* have continued to insist on reinstatement or would you have accepted offers of compensation, if sufficiently generous?

EXTENSION ACTIVITY

Write a class letter to News International and the main unions involved in the Wapping Dispute and ask for more information which gives *their* side of the dispute – because you will find that they differ greatly.

As a project, research to find out as much as you can about the dispute, and then write a report that gives the facts of the dispute. Include details of the background history leading up to it, and try to show which side you think is the most believable (if either). Finally, discuss the implications of the outcome of the dispute for the role of the unions in the future.

4.9 A factory dispute The Bertolini Brothers

A factory dispute

At the Wearside Ball-Bearing Factory there was a dispute. Bill Brown, the **Shop Steward**, insisted that the workers would accept nothing less than a 12 per cent wage increase. Montague Drake, the **Managing Director**, said that 7 per cent was the maximum that his company could afford. The union **district officials** had come to negotiate with the management, but to no avail. They suggested that the dispute be taken to **ACAS**, but the management refused.

At first **non-strike action** was taken by the workers but this was not effective, so an all-out strike was called. A **picket line** was set up and an appeal was made to other workers to **black** any products coming out. The strike was effective because the factory had a **closed shop**; thus there were very few **blacklegs**. In the end, the strike was settled with a 9 per cent wage increase in return for **increased productivity** from the workforce.

QUESTIONS

1 Explain fully the meanings of the words in **bold** (including ACAS). (10)
2 Why do you think that the management refused to go to ACAS? (3)
3 Why do you think that the workers started off with 'non-strike action'? Why do you think that this action was not effective? (4)
4 Why did the existence of a closed shop make the strike more effective? (3)
5 There are two reasons hinted at in the text why one of the long-term effects of the strike may be a loss of jobs. Find them. (5)

(25)

The Bertolini Brothers

This continues the story of the Bertolinis and their exotic Italian food factory (Unit 3, Section 3.5). Difficulties started when one of the production workers, called Paolo, tried to organise a union. He summoned the other production workers to a meeting where he delivered the following speech:

'Brothers and Sisters. The Bertolini Mafia are exploiting you. They pay you a pittance and force you to work in damp and uncomfortable conditions. Join me in the TGWU. Together we can force them to double our pay and spend money for us to work in comfort. If we stick together there are lots of ways in which we can harm their production should they refuse us. With a closed shop we could dictate our terms. Unity is strength!'

Fig. 4.18   Union worker calling for strike

The Bertolinis did not quite see things like that. Paolo was sacked and a strike followed. There was a picket line outside the factory for nine weeks, but four of the workers blacklegged and another five were recruited. In time the strike collapsed – and the Bertolinis did not even go to ACAS! Three of the workers remained members of the union, but the dream of a closed shop was lost for ever.

QUESTIONS

1 What type of worker is eligible to join the TGWU? (2)
2 What are three of the ways in which workers could 'harm production'? (3)
3 Explain the sentence, 'With a closed shop we could dictate our terms.' (4)
4 Why did the Bertolinis sack Paolo? (2)
5 Which of the Bertolinis would be responsible for dealing with the union? (N.B. Refer back to Unit 3, Section 3.5.) (2)
6 Why was there a picket line outside the factory? (3)
7 What is a blackleg? Why do you think that workers do sometimes 'scab'? (5)
8 What would have been the job of ACAS if the Bertolinis had taken the case before them? (4)
9 Write a short memorandum from the relevant Bertolini to Antonio and Mario explaining what steps could be taken to increase the workers' happiness within the firm and reduce their desire to join a union. (N.B. Refer to Sections 4.1 and 4.2.) (10)

(35)

5.1 Costs, revenues and break-even analysis

Winston Brown was very sorry when his grandmother died, but her last bequest enabled him to realise his life's ambition and start his own car-repair business. Immediately he found that he had to pay out some money – much to his disappointment! In other words he had **costs**. He had to **rent** a garage, buy **equipment**, pay **interest** on a bank loan – and all before he had repaired a single car! When he did start work he had to pay **wages** to his assistant, **electricity** bills and pay for **materials**.

Can you see the difference between the two types of cost? The first three were involved in **setting up** the business, the last three in **running** it. To put it another way the first three do not, on the whole, vary with the number of cars repaired and so are known as **fixed costs**; the last three do and so are known as **variable costs**.

Fixed costs
Rent
Equipment
Interest on loan

Variable costs
Wages
Electricity
Materials

This can be seen graphically in Fig. 5.1.

In practice it is not always easy to make the distinction. For instance, although he will have to pay his assistant overtime if a lot of work comes in, he will pay a basic wage regardless. On the other hand a lot of work may mean that he buys more equipment. Costs such as these are known as **semi-variable costs**. For simplicity, however, we will class costs only as fixed or variable in this Unit.

There would be little point in a firm incurring these costs to make the product or provide the service if it did

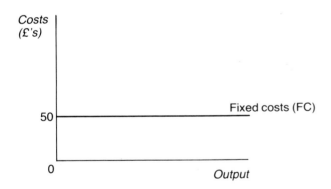

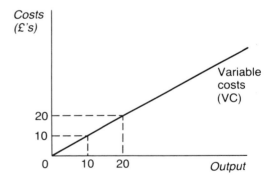

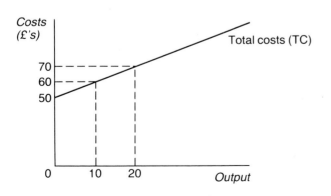

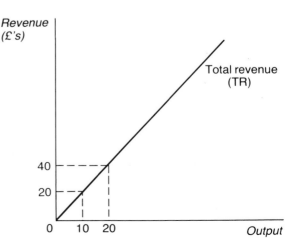

Fig. 5.1

Fig. 5.2

Output (units)	FC (£s)	VC (£s)	TC (£s)	Price (£s)	TR (£s)	Profit (£s)
0	50	0	50	2	0	−50
10		10				
20		20				
30		30				
40		40				
50		50				
60		60				
70		70				
80		80				

not hope to receive money back from selling it. This money is known as its **revenue**. So if a firm sells 100 units of a product at £2 each its total revenue is £200.

Total revenue = Quantity sold × Price

For a firm to continue in business it needs to be sure that the money it will receive for its goods or services is at least as great as the costs that it has to pay out. In other words:

Total revenue = Total costs
   or
Price × Quantity = Fixed costs + Variable costs

This is known as the **break-even point**.

If total revenue is *greater* than total costs the firm is making a **profit**. If total revenue is *less* than total costs the firm is making a **loss**.

EXERCISE

Copy and complete the table (Fig. 5.2) and remember:
(a) Fixed costs (FC) don't change with output.

(b) Total costs (TC) are fixed costs + variable costs.
(c) Total revenue (TR) is price × output.
(d) Profit = Total revenue − Total costs.

Compare your answers with the graph in Fig. 5.3.

It is also possible to calculate the break-even from far less information. (This section uses some maths. It is not too difficult so do give it a try.) Let's use the example given in the first exercise: fixed costs are £50, variable costs £1 per unit and the product can be sold for £2 per unit. What is the break-even output?

Break-even is where total revenue = total costs (TR = TC).

Total revenue is found by multiplying the quantity by the price (p × q).

Total costs are the fixed costs plus the variable costs (FC + VC).

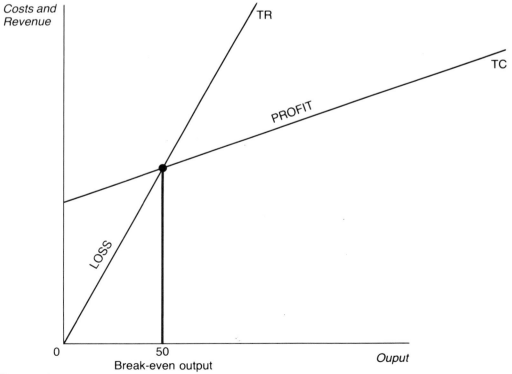

Fig. 5.3   Costs and revenue

So we can also write   TR   = TC
                    as   p × q = FC + VC

Let's call the break-even quantity X.
We can now write the equation
as $2 \times x$
or $2X = 50 + 1 \times x$
$\quad = 50 + x$

which is easily solved:
$2X - x = 50$
$x \quad = 50$

Thus the break-even output is fifty units – as we have already worked out on the table.

Given this cost and revenue structure, if the firm produces 50 units its costs will just be equal to its revenues and it will be making neither a profit nor a loss, but just breaking even.

We can prove this result by calculating total cost and total revenue at that output:

Total revenue = £2 × 50 = £100

Total cost = £50 + (£1 × 50)
       = £50 + £50
       = £100

Of course, firms wish to make a profit so they are likely to produce an output that is higher than that which is just going to break even. If they produce 60 they will have a **margin of safety** of 10 (they are producing 10 more than they need to break even).

EXERCISE

1 A firm has fixed costs of £800, variable costs of £20 per unit and can sell its output for £40 each:

   (a) Calculate the break-even output.
   (b) Verify your conclusion by calculating total revenue and total cost at that output.

2 The Wearland Tyre Company sells its tyres at a price of £10. Its fixed costs total £5,000 per annum. These include the rent of factory space, rates to the local authority and the interest that it pays to the bank for the loan for the machine that it has just bought. Its variable costs total £5 per tyre – mainly the wage bill and the cost of the rubber.

   (a) Calculate the break-even output and plot your results on a graph.
   (b) If the firm decides to produce 1,500 tyres, what is its:
       (i) margin of safety;
       (ii) annual profit?
   (c) Discuss as a group the factors which could ensure that the firm does not break even although it produces the amount that you recommend from the figures; i.e. what if it cannot sell all those tyres at £10? Report on your findings.

5.2 Accounting made simple

Costs and revenues only tell us a limited amount about the financial position of a business. More information is needed to give the full picture, as detailed financial control is necessary for the success of any business. This will become apparent as we proceed.

We saw in Unit 1, Section 1.2, that for any business to operate it needs to have certain possessions – **resources** – and those resources must be supplied by someone.

Resources owned by the firm are known as **assets**.
Some will be supplied by the owner – **capital**.
Some will be supplied by people outside the firm – **liabilities**.
Capital + Liabilities = Assets

This is known as the **accounting equation**. It must always be true because everything that the firm has must either have been supplied by the owner or from outside.

The accounting equation is expressed in the **Balance Sheet**. Let us see how this Balance Sheet is drawn up from the very beginning of a business.

Winston Brown used the money that his grandmother left him in her will to start his own car-repair business. She left him £10,000 and he immediately put it into a bank account under a business name, 'Brown's Mend-It'. This was on 1 June 1986 and he had his first Balance Sheet:

Brown's Mend-It
Balance Sheet as on 1 June 1986

	£	(Cash)	£
Capital	10,000	Assets	10,000

Cash sitting in a bank will hardly get a business moving, however. What is the first thing that Winston Brown will need to make his business operational?   Premises! This leads us to the discovery of two types of asset:

1 **Fixed assets**
   These are objects owned by the company. They do not change – buildings, vehicles, machinery.
2 **Current assets**
   These are involved in the everyday running of the company and are constantly changing – cash, stock, debtors. They are also known as **circulating** or **working capital**.

The difference between the two will become clearer as we proceed.

So Winston Brown finds a disused garage that he can obtain for £6,000. He has £10,000 in the bank so he pays out of that. How much money does that leave in the bank? This transaction took place on 6 June and so he now has a new Balance Sheet.

Brown's Mend-It
Balance Sheet as on 6 June 1986

	£		£
Capital	10,000	*Fixed assets*	
		Building	6,000
Current liabilities		*Current Assets*	
		Cash	4,000
	10,000		10,000

There are three things to note from this new Balance Sheet:

1 The *capital* is unchanged. Brown's cash has been reduced to pay for the building but he has still put the same amount of cash into the business – it is just divided between cash and buildings.
2 He now has two types of asset – *fixed* and *current*.
3 It still **balances** – every *use* of funds (assets) must have a *source* (liabilities).

In order to get the business going Brown must buy in some stock (so he can sell 'spares') – for £1,000. He decides to take advantage of the credit facilities offered by the equipment firm, however, to avoid paying straight away.

In so doing, Brown has incurred a **liability**. He now owes money to (is 'liable' to) another firm. By avoiding immediate payment he has found an additional source of funds.

Brown's Mend-It
Balance Sheet as on 9 June 1986

	£		£
Capital	10,000	Fixed assets	
		Building	6,000
Current liabilities		Current assets	
Creditor	1,000	Stock	1,000
		Cash	4,000
	11,000		11,000

The totals have changed – but it still balances!

Brown decides to sell part of his stock to another firm, as he finds that he does not need it all at this stage. He sells it for £200 and he offers credit facilities. So he now has a **debtor** which is a current asset because it is a *use* of his funds to lend them to someone else.

Brown's Mend-It
Balance Sheet as on 30 June 1986

	£		£
Capital	10,00	Fixed assets	
		Building	6,000
Current liabilities		Current assets	
Creditor	1,000	Stock	800
		Debtor	200
		Cash	4,000
	11,000		11,000

You will notice that every transaction affects *two* items on the Balance Sheet. That is why it is called **double-entry accounting**.

EXERCISE

Enter the following transactions for *Brown's Mend-It*. Remember that it is a double-entry system so you must change two items each time. Draw up a fresh Balance Sheet after each question.

(a) Brown sold goods for £100 and was paid immediately by cash.
(b) Brown pays £400 in part-payment of the money that he owes.
(c) Brown receives £150 of the money that he is owed.

Explain the two items that you have changed each time.

5.3 Profit and cash flow

We have not yet looked in detail at a most important aspect of business finance – the profit. As we saw when we looked at break-even analysis (Section 5.1) the profit is the difference between the *total revenue* earned from the sales of the goods and the *total cost* of their production. The accountant has two main measures of profit, however. Consider the following example.

Winston Brown finds that car repairs are not very profitable and a friend advises him to branch out into selling second-hand cars. His monthly sales from the first six months work out as follows:

Jan. £500; Feb. £600; Mar. £600; Apr. £700; May £600; June £500.

Thus the total value of his sales in the first six months is £3,500.

He has bought in 30 cars for £100 each at a rate of five per month, but has only sold 20 of them. So the total 'cost of sales' works out at £3,000 *minus* the value of the stock that is left (which is, of course, available to be sold); that is, £1,000 (taking the stock value to be the cost price of the cars).

We can easily calculate from this his **gross profit**:

Trading Account for Winston Brown as at 1 July 1987

	£	£
Sales		3,500
Less cost of goods sold:		
Purchases (30 × £10)	3,000	
Less Stock (10 × £10)	1,000	
		2,000
Gross profit		1,500

$$\text{i.e. Gross profit} = \text{Sales} - \text{Cost of sales}$$
$$= £3,500 - £2,000$$
$$= £1,500$$

Obviously Brown is going to have other expenses apart from buying the cars. He will have **rent** on the building (£30 per month); **wages** (£40 per month), **heating** (£10 per month) and **general expenses** (£5 per month). He may also decide to buy a vehicle for business purposes which could cost him £1,000. He will not take *all* the vehicle cost off his profit immediately because it will last him for a number of years. Instead he will 'write off' or **depreciate** it by a certain amount each year. If he expects it to last for eight years and have a 'scrap value' of £200 he has £800 to write off over eight years – £100 per year.

We must deduct these expenses from his gross profit to arrive at a figure for **net profit**.

Profit and Loss Account for Winston Brown as at 1 July 1987

	£	£
Gross profit		1,500
Rent (6 × £30)	180	
Wages (6 × £40)	240	
Heat (6 × £10)	60	
General expenses (6 × £5)	30	
Depreciation (½ × £100)	50	
		560
Net profit		940

Does this mean cash in hand?

We have calculated that Brown has made a net profit of £940. This means that, over the first six months, the value of his sales is worth £940 more than his costs. It does *not* necessarily mean that he has £940 worth of cash in his hands, however. There are a number of reasons why these figures – for *profit* and for *cash* – may be different:

He must have had some money to start with – some *capital*; in his case this was £500.

He had to pay out £1,000 cash for the vehicle rather than £50 depreciation charged on the profit and loss account.

Most businesses have to allow their customers some period of *credit*. Brown has been buying in 5 cars per month but he has been paying for them *one month later*. He also allows his customers one month's credit.

The cash flow budget

From the information given we can draw up a **cash flow budget** showing how much cash he actually receives and pays out each month. For instance in month 1 (January) he starts off with the £500 capital that he started the business with. He does not receive any money for sales because he allows his customers one month's credit. So the money for sales in any month will be the value of sales in the *previous* month (£500 in February, £600 in March, etc.). His rent, wages, heat and light and general expenses are the same each month. So are his supplies – although again he pays nothing in the first month because he is allowed a month's credit. He pays £1,000 for the vehicle, including tax and insurance for the first year, in the first month. By taking the **total outflow from the total inflow** each month we can calculate how much money he has at the end of each month – the **closing balance**. (See Fig. 5.4.)

This leads us to a rather surprising discovery. Despite making a profit of £940 during his first six months' trading, Brown has spent £510 more than he has – in other words

he has an **overdraft**. This is not at all unusual for a business, particularly when it is starting out. Banks are usually happy to allow an 'overdraft facility' up to a certain level, as long as they believe that the business has every prospect of paying it off in time. In this case the bank has given Brown an overdraft of £1,000 which he has not exceeded – and, if you look at the *trend* of his monthly deficit, it is decreasing (getting less) each month as sales increase. It was really a way of enabling Brown to buy the vehicle. The bank could have given Brown a fixed **loan** instead, which he could pay off in instalments. They would have charged less interest for this than they would on the overdraft but he would not have had the **flexibility** that the overdraft allows. If he has an unexpected expense, or a bad month for sales, he can 'dip into it' – up to the limit set.

Cash flow budgets are widely used in business to **forecast** firms' likely need for cash over a period of time and so enable them to arrange for overdrafts or loans if it looks as if they are going to need them. Thus 'cash flow problems' – shortage of cash at certain times – can be anticipated and avoided.

EXERCISE

Draw up another cash flow budget on the assumption that Winston Brown has to allow his customers *two* months' credit although he is allowed just one month by his suppliers. If he is still allowed an overdraft of £1,000, write a note on what problems this would cause him and how he might get round them.

Fig. 5.4

	Jan.	Feb.	Mar.	Apr.	May	June
A: Opening balance	£500	−£585	−£670	−£655	−£640	−£525
B: Sales	0	£500	£600	£600	£700	£600
C: Total inflow (A+B)	£500	£−85	£−70	£−55	£60	£75
D: Rent	£30	£30	£30	£30	£30	£30
E: Wages	£40	£40	£40	£40	£40	£40
F: Heat and light	£10	£10	£10	£10	£10	£10
G: General expenses	£5	£5	£5	£5	£5	£5
H: Supplies	£0	£500	£500	£500	£500	£500
I: Vehicle	£1,000	0	0	0	0	0
J: Total outflow (D+E+F+G+H+I)	£1,085	£585	£585	£585	£585	£585
K: Closing balance (C−J)	(−£585)	(−£670)	(−£655)	(−£640)	(−£525)	(−£510)

5.4 The balance sheet

In practice firms do not draw up a Balance Sheet after every transaction (as we did in Section 5.2) but at the end of a financial period, usually a year. Winston Brown wishes to assess his situation after six months, however, and so wants a Balance Sheet to show him his *sources* of funds and the *uses* to which he has put them.

You will notice that this Balance Sheet is set out slightly differently from those that you have seen so far. It contains exactly the same information: the sources of funds – Capital and Liabilities, and the uses to which they are put – Fixed and Current Assets. Most companies set out their Balance Sheet in *vertical* form as below, however. It is thought to be easier to follow.

Balance Sheet of J. Brown as at 1 July 1987

	£	£
Fixed assets		
Vehicle	1,000	
Less Depreciation	50	
	950	
Current assets		
Stock	1,000	
Debtors	500	
	1,500	2,450
Current liabilities		
Creditors	500	
Overdraft	510	
	1,010	
Net current assets*	490	
Total assets – Current liabilities	1,440	
Represented by		
Capital and Reserves:		
Capital		
Capital	500	
Profit & Loss Account	940	
	1,440	2,450

As you can see, the basic principle of the Balance Sheet still applies – Fixed and Current assets (use) is equal to capital, profit and liabilities (source).

* Net Current assets = Current assets – Current liabilities

EXERCISE

To test that you have followed the argument of the unit, write a sentence or two on each of the items in the Balance Sheet shown here, explaining how the value was found.

To what use can we put this Balance Sheet?

Apart from showing us the sources of funds for a business and the use to which those funds have been put, we can find other useful information about the business. For example, Winston Brown may wish to know the total amount of capital that is employed in the business. This will tell him the value of all the assets at his disposal:

$$Employed\ capital = Fixed\ assets + Current\ assets$$
$$= £950 + £1,500$$
$$= £2,450$$

He may wish to know the total amount of capital that is owned by the business when all the debts have been paid off:

$$Capital\ owned = Employed\ capital - Current\ liabilities$$
$$= £2,450 - £1,010$$
$$= £1,440$$

He may wish to know the amount of capital left working in the business when the debts have been re-paid:

$$Net\ working\ capital = Current\ assets - Current\ liabilities$$
$$= £1,500 - £1,010$$
$$= £490$$

N.B. You will notice that these last two ratios were calculated on the Balance Sheet. This is the practice that most companies follow when drawing up their Balance Sheets.

We can also join information from the Balance Sheet with information from the Trading and Profit and Loss Accounts. Firms are very keen to know how quickly their stocks of goods are 'turned over' or actually sold. In the six months Brown's **turnover** is £3,500 – that is the value of the goods that he has sold. His 'average stock' is his stock at the beginning (£0) plus his stock at the end (£1,000) divided by two = £500.

$$Rate\ of\ turnover = \frac{Turnover}{Average\ stock\ at\ cost\ price}$$

$$= \frac{£3,500}{£500}$$

$$= \frac{7}{-}$$

He will also want to know how well he has used the capital that he put in at the beginning of the year. He does that by comparing the value of that capital with the profit that he has earned:

$$Return\ on\ capital\ invested\ =\ \frac{Net\ profit}{Capital\ at\ start\ of\ year}$$

$$=\ \frac{£940}{£500}$$

$$=\ \underline{1.88}$$

Finally he may well wish to know how much money – or assets that can be turned easily into money – that he has to meet the debts that he has. This is called measuring his **liquidity**. Cash is the most 'liquid' asset because it can be spent just as it is. Debtors are slightly less liquid – the money has to be 'chased'. Stock is the least liquid because it has to be turned into a finished product and sold before it can be turned into cash. There are two ratios that measure liquidity:

$$Current\ ratio\ =\ \frac{Current\ assets}{Current\ liabilities}$$

$$=\ \frac{£1,500}{£1,010}$$

$$=\ \underline{1.48}$$

A slightly 'stricter' test leaves out stock from current assets for the reason that we said – it cannot be easily turned into cash:

$$Acid\ test\ ratio\ =\ \frac{Liquid\ assets\ (Current\ assets\ -\ Stock)}{Current\ liabilities}$$

$$=\ \frac{£500}{£1,010}$$

$$=\ \underline{0.49}$$

You might well ask how you can tell if these are good or bad figures? This is a good question! There is no 'right' figure for any one of them – it depends very much on the company, its size and the position that it is in. However, there are one or two things that stand out from these figures. The return on capital invested is a high percentage by anyone's standards and suggests that the initial capital has been well used. On the other hand, the liquidity figures look less good. We know that he has an overdraft at the bank which is likely to mean that he is short of 'ready cash'. A current ratio of around 2 and an acid test ratio of around 1 are usually considered reasonable. In this case both are well below, which would mean trouble if the money that he owes should suddenly be required. The figures can only be really appreciated if they are compared on a year-to-year basis so that a **trend** can be found – in which *direction* are things moving? That is outside the scope of this book but you could try tackling it by using the techniques that you have learnt in this unit.

5.5 The Bertolini Brothers

The Bertolini brothers discovered that pizzas were selling better than any other type of food and so they decided to concentrate on them. They have a big argument as to how many they should produce and the price that they should charge. Everybody joins in. This is an excerpt:

Frederico: Look! With our overheads of £10,000 and our variable costs of £10 per box then we must aim to sell at least 5,000 boxes because, with the market as it is at the moment, we cannot possibly charge more than £12 per box. If we sell any less at that price we make a loss.

Franco: Faint heart! We can get £15 for each box. I know it! And if we do then we can make £15,000 profit on those 5,000 boxes. If we make 7,000, which I am sure that we could sell, who knows how much profit we could make?

QUESTIONS

1 Explain the difference between overheads and variable costs, giving two examples of each. (5)
2 Both Frederico and Franco are correct with their figures. Prove it. (15)
3 How much profit could they make if they sold 7,000 boxes at £15? (5)
4 Discuss the factors that will influence whether they are in fact able to sell pizzas successfully at the higher price. (5)

(30)

It is the end of the first financial year for the company since incorporation. It is Maria's job to draw up the accounts. She has the following information.

The capital put in at the beginning of the year was £5,000; contrary to even Franco's expectations they have managed to sell 10,000 boxes at £15 per box. As you have already been told the cost of making each box is £10 and the overheads of £10,000 are counted as expenses; they break down into £6,000 wages, £2,000 power and £2,000 general expenses. The wage bill is monthly, the power and expense bills are quarterly.

The building was bought at the beginning of the year for £20,000 and the machinery was bought for £5,000. As shareholders the Bertolinis expect their dividend; there are ten of them and they are owed £500 each to be paid at the end of the year. The accounts are drawn up just before the end of December and at that point the company is owed £5,000 for pizzas sold in that month and owes suppliers £5000 – again for goods bought in that month. Otherwise all payments are prompt and even. At the time of drawing up the accounts the company has a stock worth £5,000. Receipts for boxes of pizzas are monthly. Payments for supplies are quarterly.

Your task

1 Use this information to draw up:
   (a) a trading account showing gross profit;
   (b) a profit and loss account showing net profit;
   (c) a cash flow budget;
   (d) a balance sheet.
2 Prepare a report from the Accountant to the Managing Director on the financial position of the company, using any ratios that you think appropriate. Put in any recommendations that you think necessary to improve the financial running of the company.

6.1 The consumer as decision maker in the market

What is a market?

A market is where buyers and sellers of any commodity are in contact with each other. It need not be a place – modern communications are such that they can be in contact from opposite ends of the earth via telephones, telex, teleprinters, etc. Thus the term 'market' covers such different activities as selling fruit and vegetables in a street market and selling cargo on ships to people in Australia from a London office.

What is a consumer?

A consumer is someone who has the desire to purchase a commodity and the purchasing power to make that desire effective. In other words it is someone who purchases goods and services.

The United Kingdom basically has what is termed a **market economy**. This means that some firms are privately owned by groups of shareholders rather than the government and that those firms base their decisions about what they produce and the price at which they will sell it on the reactions of 'the market', i.e. those who purchase their product; only in that way can they hope to produce at a profit and thus persuade people to finance their activities by buying their shares.

It is usually reasonable to assume that the lower the price of a product the more people will want to buy it – and vice versa. Thus if we plot a number of different points showing the relationship between price and quantity demanded, the result is shown in Fig. 6.1. If we then consider the relationship between price and quantity supplied we find that the opposite relationship holds – the higher the price that the firm expects to receive the more will it be prepared to supply (Fig. 6.2). The price and quantity supplied and demanded that will finally emerge will be found at the point at which supply and demand are equal (Fig. 6.3).

Let us imagine that the firm tries to charge a price that is higher than this **equilibrium**. As can be seen in Fig. 6.4, supply (S) is greater than demand (D). This means that firms will lower their prices in order to try to get rid of their surplus stock. If, on the other hand, the price is lower than the equilibrium, then demand will be greater than supply (Fig. 6.5). Firms will increase their prices to try to ration out the scarce goods.

Thus, in both cases, the price is moving towards the equilibrium and at that point it will stop. That is what 'equilibrium' means – the level from which there is no tendency to change.

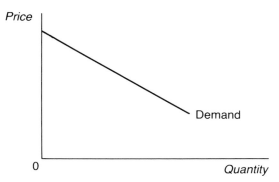

Fig. 6.1

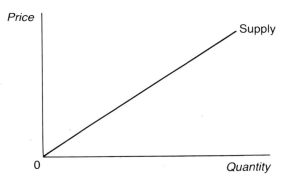

Fig. 6.2

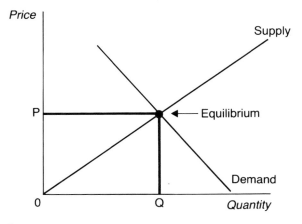

Fig. 6.3

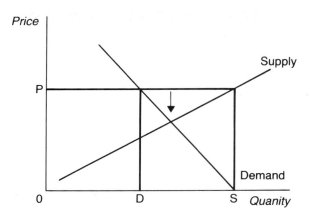

Fig. 6.4

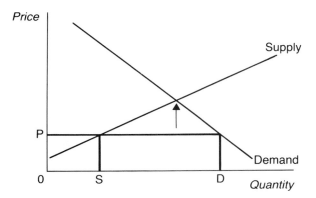

Fig. 6.5

From this analysis it is therefore possible to work out not only the price at which the product will sell but also the *quantity* that will be supplied and demanded. By deciding, as a group, to buy at a certain price the consumers have used their spending power to bring goods on to the market. This is known as **consumer sovereignty** – consumers acting as decision makers in the market. If they did not want a product they would not purchase it, and so it would not be worth while for the firm to produce it.

Demand curve

The line showing how demand changes as price changes is known as a **demand curve**. As you will see, it shows the amount of a product that is wanted at different prices. It assumes that other things that might affect the demand for a product are constant – in real life they may not be, of course. Let us imagine that you are thinking of buying a record. It will not just be the *price* that will help you decide whether to buy it or not. There will also be the amount of *money* that you have, whether you *like* it or not, whether you have seen it *advertised*. So an increase in demand at all

prices could be caused by any – or all – of the following factors:

- an increase in income;
- a shift of taste in favour of the product;
- a successful advertising campaign for the product.

The opposite will *reduce* demand and so shift that demand. Therefore, an increase in demand will shift the demand curve to the *right*. The opposite will reduce demand and so shift the demand curve to the *left*.

Supply curve

This is the line that shows how supply changes as price changes. Again, other things will affect how much of a product can be produced apart from the price: how modern and efficient the technology is; how high the costs – wages, rent, rates, materials, etc. – are; how many factors of production – workers, machinery, etc. – the firm can get its hands on. So an increase in supply at all prices could be caused by:

- an improvement in technology;
- a reduction in costs;
- an increase in the supply of the factors of production.

The opposite will *reduce* supply and so shift the supply curve to the *left*.

EXERCISE

(a) Use the figures in Fig. 6.6 to produce a graph with axes clearly labelled.
(b) What is the equilibrium price and quantity? Explain your answer.
(c) If price were 2 how much excess demand would there be? What would you do if you were the firm?
(d) How would you describe the situation if price were 9?
(e) Imagine that the firm has run a successful advertising campaign and has done so well in persuading more people to buy their goods that demand has increased by 2 at all prices. Draw the new situation on your original graph. What is the new price and quantity?
(f) Is your answer to (e) what you would expect? Explain your answer.

Fig. 6.6

Price (£'s)	Quantity demanded	Quantity supplied
1	10	1
2	9	2
3	8	3
4	7	4
5	6	5
6	5	5
7	4	6
8	3	7
9	2	8
10	1	10

6.2 Market research

Jean and Ron worked together in an office and they both hated it. They discovered that they shared an interest in cooking, however, and the idea came to them of setting up a restaurant together. They each had relatives who were prepared to lend them some money and they managed to persuade the bank manager that they were worth a loan. Before going ahead and rushing into anything they decided that it would be a good idea to find out what sort of restaurant would be most popular – in other words, they decided to carry out some **market research**.

They devised a **questionnaire** for local people to fill in. This, as the name suggests, is a set of questions that is designed to provide specific information. The questionnaire must be very carefully drawn up to get just the information that is required. It must also be borne in mind that people are not prepared to spend a long time filling it in so it must be easy to understand and complete.

EXERCISE

Jean and Ron developed two questionnaires. Look at each carefully and say which you think would be most suitable. Explain your answer fully.

Questionnaire 1
Full name:
Address:
Date of Birth:
Occupation:
Sex:
Do you eat out at restaurants at present?
If the answer to the above is 'yes', what type of restaurant do you usually go to?
Would you be interested in trying a new restaurant?
If the answer to the above is 'yes', what type of food would interest you?

Questionnaire 2
We are thinking of opening a new restaurant in this town. Your co-operation would be appreciated in answering a few questions.
Do you go to a restaurant: once a week
                            once a month
                            less frequently
                            more frequently
Do you usually go with: your husband/wife
                         boyfriend/girlfriend
                         friends of the same sex
                         relations
                         others
What type of restaurant do you most often
go to: English
         French
         Chinese
         Indian
         other (please specify)

What is the most important factor in your decision as to which restaurant to go to: type of food
                               quality of food
                               price
                               other (please specify)
If a new restaurant were to open what type of food would you prefer that it served?
If it were to serve the type of food that you have just mentioned would you be prepared to try it?
Thank you for your co-operation.

Jean carried out most of the **primary research**. This means that she actually stopped people in the street and asked them the questions. Ron sat behind a desk and analysed the results. In other words he used the completed questionnaires to work out if it was worth them even thinking of opening a restaurant; if it was, what sort of food they should sell; and whether they should concentrate on 'quality' food and not worry about price or concentrate on low-price, good-value meals. This is known as carrying out the **secondary research**.

There were a number of rules that Jean and Ron needed to follow when they were carrying out their market research and evaluating it afterwards:

- Try to ensure that the group of people to whom they spoke – the **sample** – were as **representative** as possible of their **target population** – the people they hoped would use their restaurant. In other words they should avoid *bias*. There would be no point in interviewing a lot of children who were not likely to be going out for a meal on their own.

Fig. 6.7   Jean at work

- Remember that even if they avoid bias as far as possible and have a representative sample the results still may not be accurate because they have not interviewed everybody. There are organisations that take great trouble to find out how people are going to vote in General Elections by carrying out opinion **polls** and they are very careful to ask a 'representative sample' of electors of different ages, sex, social class, etc. They cannot ask more than about 1,500 people in any one poll, however, and there are 25 million people who vote in General Elections – so, not surprisingly, they sometimes get the answer wrong. The same is true of any questionnaire; it is bound to be liable to error and that should always be borne in mind when the results are analysed.

Summary

- Market research is carried out to assess the likely demand for a product and the factors that are most likely to persuade people to buy it. It is a good idea to carry this out before finally deciding what to produce.
- A questionnaire is the most usual way of discovering the information that is required.

- The questionnaire should be relevant, to the point and easy to fill in.
- As far as possible a representative sample should be questioned and bias should be avoided.
- When analysing the results care should be taken to remember that the survey can never be fully representative and so is liable to error.

ACTIVITY

Imagine that you are going to start a school enterprise. You are thinking of making cushions but you are not sure if they will sell, what sort of filling would be most popular and what colour will sell best; you have found that it will be far cheaper if you use only one colour.

In groups, design a suitable questionnaire and then hold a class discussion to compare the questions. Choose the best questionnaire to carry out the survey around school. Analyse your results and discuss what you have found out. Perhaps you actually could form an enterprise to make cushions?

6.3 Advertising

The results of their questionnaire convinced Jean and Ron that there *was* a market for a new restaurant in the town and that their best bet was to specialise in medium-priced, good-quality, traditional English food. They acquired premises and equipment and set about planning just how they were going to launch their venture. They quickly decided that there was little point in opening unless people already knew about them and what they had to offer – otherwise they would be standing looking at empty tables every night. So they decided that a very high priority was an **advertising** campaign.

Advertising has two main aspects to it:

1 letting people know that the product or service is available. This is usually known as **informative** advertising.
2 trying to persuade people to buy the product or service. This is known as **persuasive** advertising.

In practice, of course, most advertisements involve elements both of information and persuasion.

There are a number of different ways to advertise – these are known as advertising **media**. Jean and Ron had to decide which **medium** to use. There were two considerations that they had to bear in mind:

1 which form was the most appropriate for their business;
2 which form they could afford to purchase.

EXERCISE

1 Below is a list of some of the different advertising media. Try to find out the cost 'per word' for each of them (per minute for radio and television). In groups, divide the list among yourselves and each person can find out specific facts, such as target audience, numbers of people likely to see the advertisement, how to place an advertisement in each medium, etc.

Shop windows	Regional television
Leaflets	National television
Billboards	National newspapers
Local newspapers	Specialist magazines
Local radio	Public transport

2 If Jean and Ron have £500 to spend on advertising, write a memorandum advising them how to spend it, costing your advice precisely.
3 Design a poster to advertise their restaurant, based on the information that you have been given about the sort of service that they intend to provide.

Not everybody is convinced that advertising is a good thing, however. Jean was discussing it with one of her friends in the office, just before she gave up her job.

Freda: Just look at these adverts all over this magazine. Doesn't it make you sick. I buy this to read the articles, not to be bombarded with stupid adverts that insult my intelligence and try to persuade me to buy things that I don't really want and would never have thought of otherwise.

Jean: Well, don't forget that if it wasn't for the revenue that the adverts provide, your magazine probably wouldn't exist at all. You don't think that the sales revenue is enough to keep them going, do you? Anyway, nobody is forcing you to read them or to buy anything. It is purely up to you.

Freda: Look, Jean, you know as well as I do that people are influenced more than they realise by advertisements. I've found myself humming the *Fruity Bar* jingle for the last couple of months – even though I've tried to stop myself! Look at the way that advertisements help to stereotype people; why is it always women who appear in washing-powder adverts, for example? Don't men ever do the washing? Basically, I believe that all this advertising is a tremendous waste of effort and money; why not do away with it and sell better-quality products at lower prices?

Fig. 6.8

Jean: People wouldn't know what was available, that's why. There is no doubt that advertising keeps sales higher than they would otherwise have been. People's jobs and livelihoods depend on that. People like the choice that advertising gives them. They like the bit of 'glamour' that it brings into their lives. Don't you think that life would be very dull if we bought one standard type of product that was sold in a brown paper bag? I suppose you think that nice packaging is a 'waste of money' as well?

Freda: Well, I certainly think that it is overdone at the moment. The aim of advertising is to persuade people that your product is different and so is worth buying over the others. Sometimes this may be the case, but don't you think it a little odd to have all those advertisements for different washing powders when they are practically all produced by just two large companies? Advertising is rarely truthful even if it is not allowed to lie. It creates a world of illusion and I don't think that is healthy.

Jean: You'll never get rid of it, I'll tell you that. As long as you have different firms producing different goods they will try to persuade people to buy their goods. Life is like that – and the world would be a more miserable place if you had your way . . .

FOR DISCUSSION

Read through the above extract with others in your group and discuss the arguments that have been brought up in favour of and against advertising. Draw up a list of the arguments under the two headings. State which side *you* favour and why.

EXTENSION ACTIVITY

Think back to the cushions that your class could make as part of an enterprise activity (see Section 6.2). Imagine that you have a budget of £50 to advertise the cushions around school and the surrounding neighbourhood. Plan your advertising campaign, finding out the exact costs of the materials to make posters and the outlets that you choose. Explain your decisions and make out a costing sheet.

6.4 Rules of advertising

We have looked at the reasons why firms advertise, the advantages that they can gain from it and some of the ways in which they carry it out. A moment's thought would tell us that there are many dangers in advertising and that there must be careful rules about how it can be carried out – the *do's* and *dont's*. After all, if there were no rules advertisers could claim anything about their product and the customers would discover that they had been misled only after they had handed over the money – by which time it would be too late.

All advertising is bound by the **British Code of Advertising Practice** and this is upheld by the **Advertising Standards Authority (ASA)** which actually ensures that it is carried out. The basic catch-phrase is that all advertisements should be 'legal, decent, honest and truthful':

- **Legal** – advertisements must contain nothing that breaks the law.
- **Decent** – advertisements must not cause unnecessary offence to a significant number of people who see the advertisement.
- **Honest** – advertisements should not take advantage of the customers' lack of knowledge to act in a way that is not in the customers' interests.
- **Truthful** – advertisements should not, 'whether by inaccuracy, ambiguity, exaggeration, omission or otherwise', mislead customers about the product.

In addition to being legal, decent, honest and truthful the Code states that advertisements should be prepared with a sense of responsibility to the consumer and society and that they should conform to the principles of fair

Fig. 6.9

competition that are accepted in business. If a member of the public believes that an advertisement breaks the Code, he or she can write to the ASA, giving the following information:

- the name of the company that is advertising;
- the name of the paper or magazine that ran the advertisement, or where the poster was seen;
- the date of the advertisement;
- exactly what the person thinks is wrong with the advertisement;
- if possible enclose a copy of the advertisement.

If the ASA decides that the advertisement goes against the Code the advertiser will be told to stop running the advertisement.

EXERCISE

Young Billy Brown saw the advertisement shown in Fig. 6.9. He rushed out and immediately bought the space gun with money that he had been saving for his holidays.

Why do you think he did this?

His mother was very annoyed, so she wrote to the Advertising Standards Authority and received the letter shown in Fig. 6.10 in reply.

The ASA asked the **agency** that had designed the advertisement to withdraw it, on the grounds that it broke the following rule: 'No advertisement should cause children to believe that they will be inferior to other children, or unpopular with them, if they do not buy a particular product or have it bought for them.'

1 Do you think that this is a good rule to have? Explain your answer.
2 Re-design the Ace Space Gun advertisement so that it does *not* go against the Code but still makes the product appear attractive to children.

The Advertising Standards Authority
Brook House, 2–16 Torrington Place, London WC1E 7HN. Telephone 01–580 5555 (9 lines)
Telex: No. 27950 MONOREF G 1020

Mrs R Brown
92 Didsbury Terrace
Newtown
GLAMORGAN

Please quote in all correspondence:
ASA/83/2568/BS

Dear Mrs Brown

Re: Ace Space Guns

Thank you for drawing our attention to the Ace Space gun advertisement in your son's comic. We have written to the advertising agency concerned and are dealing with the matter.

Yours sincerely

Beryl Smith (Ms)

Chairman: Professor Lord McGregor of Durris
Director General: Peter Thomson
Members of Council M. C. J. Barnes, Esq MA Dame Josephine Barnes DBE. FRCP FRCS FRCOG Lady Elizabeth Cavendish MVO JP E. G. Court, Esq Prof the Rev Canon G. R. Dunstan A. M. Fisher Esq., MA The Baroness Lockwood Miss Patricia Mann, FIPA, FCAM A. E. Pitcher, Esq. FIPA FCAM Mrs Rachel Waterhouse, CBE. PhD
The Advertising Standards Authority Limited Registration No: 733214 England
A non-profit making company by guarantee

Fig. 6.10

6.5 The product life cycle

A central idea in the analysis of the marketing strategy of a firm is that of the **product life cycle.** Imagine the following situation.

Chris Boffin, the head of the **Research and Development** Department at Crunchy Crisps Ltd, came up with a brilliant idea; chocolate flavoured crisps. He worked out the ingredients needed to produce these crisps and believed that he could be on to a 'winner' – the combination of crisps and chocolate should really catch on by appealing both to the sweet and the savoury tooth. There were one or two little problems to be sorted out in the production but he believed that these were not difficult.

The first issue of the new crisps came out on 1st January. Boffin was aware that they were not yet 'technically perfect' and so these were really the **prototype** of the new product. In order that people should know about them there was an extensive advertising campaign; nevertheless, because the product was both new and slightly imperfect, sales grew only slowly during the first three months – 10,000 packets in January, 12,000 in February and 13,000 in March. These were sold at 10p each; as the initial costs were £50,000 and each packet cost another 5p to produce you can see that Crunchy Crisps Ltd did not make much money in that time – in fact they lost money.

By the end of March they had ironed out the technical problems, however, and the advertising campaign had taken effect – 'munch the chocolatey crunch' was being sung up and down the land. This led to sales of 25,000 in April, 40,000 in May, 65,000 in June and 100,000 in July. The executives at Crunchy Crisps were rubbing their hands with glee in the expectation that sales would continue to rise at this rate indefinitely – or at least for a very long time. They were to receive an unpleasant surprise the following month when the figures were only 105,000; not bad in themselves, but hardly the rate of increase that they were expecting in view of the previous rapid rise. The Marketing Department held an emergency meeting and it was agreed that there should be a further boost to advertising along with a slight change in the 'image' of the product; possibly people were beginning to think 'chocolate crisps' were unhealthy so it was emphasised that they were, in fact, low in sugar and salt (not easy for chocolate crisps). September sales rose to 115,000 and October's to 120,000, but really the 'writing was on the wall'. In November sales actually *fell* to 105,000 and in December they were down to 80,000. Plans were made by the firm to 'diversify', i.e. investigate other products and the 'line' was discontinued in the new year.

EXERCISE

1 Using the figures given for sales in each month draw a **line graph** comparing sales in each month. Put the 'time' axis on the bottom and the 'sales' up the side.

2 Calculate the profit and/or loss for: (a) the first three months; (b) the whole year.

The graph in Fig. 6.11 shows a shape similar to the one you have drawn to show the sales of the chocolate flavoured crisps. This is called a product life cycle and you should be able to see that it is divided into four parts:

1 **Introductory** (January–March)
This is when the product is first introduced. It is not well known and there may well be technical problems. Thus sales will at best grow slowly. The Marketing Department will be working flat out to advertise the product and the Research and Development Department will be trying to iron out the technical problems.

2 **Growth** (April–July)
The problems mentioned above have been solved and the sales are gaining momentum. It is during this period that the product is likely to repay the initial investment. Marketing and Research can, to a certain extent, 'step back'; it is up to the Production Department to ensure that they can keep up with the rising demand for the product.

3 **Maturity** (August–October)

The 'novelty' has worn off, the market has stopped expanding and sales are beginning to 'peak'. In an attempt to stop this process the Marketing Department may well try to increase the advertising, the Research Department may try to refine and improve the product and the Accounts Department may decide that a price cut is a good idea.

4 **Decline** (November–December)

If the above strategies do not work then sales will soon begin to fall. It is likely that, at this point, the firm will give up on the product – at least in its present form – and attempt to 'diversify' into other areas. Chris Boffin needs another idea . . .

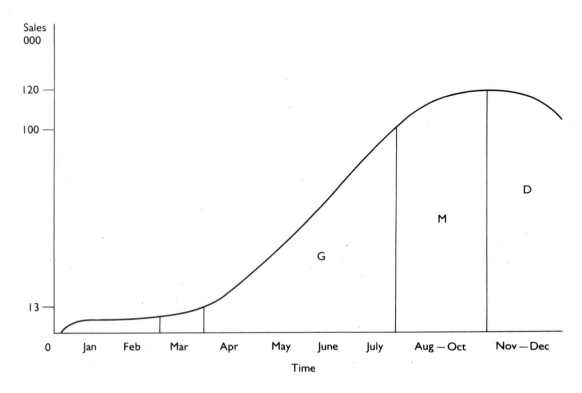

Fig. 6.11   The product life cycle

6.6 Economies of scale

A firm will find that, as it produces more and becomes larger, it can produce more cheaply. This can be seen in two different ways:

Average cost of production

One machine may be designed for use by six workers. Thus as the number of workers increases – at least up to six – the **average cost of production** will fall. We have looked at the different types of cost that firms have to pay – *fixed* and *variable* – which, added together, make up *total cost*. As the name suggests the *average* cost per worker is the total cost of production divided by the number of workers.

EXERCISE

Look at the table in Fig. 6.12.

Fill in the gaps and chart the results for average costs onto graph paper – showing average costs against the number of workers. What happens to the average cost of production as the number of workers rises? What happens when the sixth worker is employed?

As long as average costs are *falling* a firm is benefiting from **economies of scale.** When they start *rising* they are suffering from **diseconomies of scale.** Can you think of the reasons *why* costs might start rising again when the sixth person is employed? (*Hint:* Think about what happens to the meal when too many people start to crowd into the kitchen!)

The graph in Fig 6.13 shows what this situation may look like.

Economies of scale

Let us compare two similar businesses of very different sizes – a corner shop and a supermarket. We will look at four areas – machinery, purchasing, borrowing money and the different types of goods available for sale.

1 Machinery

If a small shop wishes to buy a bacon slicer it will represent a larger proportion of its total income than would be the

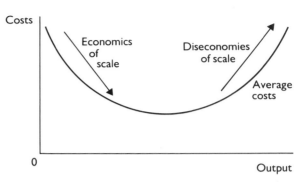

Fig. 6.13

case for a supermarket. The supermarket will be better known to the suppliers because it buys more from them. Further, when the bacon slicer arrives the chances are that it will be used for a greater proportion of the time in the supermarket than it will be in the small shop. These are known as **technical economies of scale.**

2 Purchasing

The previous point really leads into this one. The supermarket will 'buy in bulk' all its supplies. This is more convenient and profitable for the suppliers who will therefore tend to offer **discounts.** Thus the average costs of buying supplies will be lower for the supermarket which will then be able to sell them at a lower price – **marketing economies of scale.**

3 Borrowing money

When a bank manager receives an application for a loan he or she will look at such things as the income that you already have, your prospects for earning income in the future and the 'security' or 'collateral' that you can offer as a guarantee that you will be able to re-pay the loan. On all of these counts the supermarket is likely to be a better prospect than the corner shop and so will find it easier to borrow money at lower rates of interest – **financial economies of scale.**

Fig. 6.12

Number of workers	Fixed cost (£'s)	Variable cost (£'s)	Total cost (£'s)	Average cost (£'s)
1	10	5	15	15
2	10	6	16	8
3		7		
4		10		
5		15		
6		24		

4 Goods available for sale

There is no comparison between the choice of goods available at a corner shop and those available at a supermarket. Apart from the advantages that the latter has for the shopper it also means that if one range is not very successful in a supermarket it is likely to be made up for by sales in other areas. A small shop has no such 'cushion' and the failure of a particular range is likely to be far more significant – the **risk-bearing economy of scale.**

Despite all this small shops do continue – indeed, many people prefer them. To see why, we need only to look at some of the 'bad points' of large supermarkets:

- Assistants are unlikely to know the customers, may well be less 'friendly' and customers' 'individual needs' will therefore not be catered for.
- The assistants are less likely to 'identify' with the supermarket than they would a small shop and this may lead to dissatisfaction and strikes.
- Communication round the supermarket may be poor and the workers are unlikely to know what is going on in other departments.

- There will be a greater **division of labour** in a supermarket – each worker will do just one job rather than 'a bit of everything', as in a smaller store. This is likely to lead to boredom and resentment.

These are problems in all large businesses, not just supermarkets, and are known as diseconomies of scale – in other words, the bad side of large businesses.

EXERCISE

In each of the following cases identify the type of economy of scale (or diseconomy of scale) that is being described:
(a) The car components firm that sells at a discount to large firms.
(b) The finance house that offers a 2½ per cent discount on all loans over £25,000.
(c) The discount on the large lathe.
(d) Lever Brothers sell five different types of washing powder.
(e) Ford Motor Company have a 'crockery smashing room' for their workers. Why?

6.7 How firms grow

We have just seen some of the advantages of large firms through looking at economies of scale. We now need to see how firms actually manage to grow. The 'obvious' way is through **success** – increasing sales by providing the customers with the product or service that they want at a price that they are prepared to pay. In this way a company may begin as a sole trader and end up as a limited company. There are a number of other ways in which firms may grow, however.

Integration

This involves joining up with another firm in the same, or a related, form of business. There are two types of integration:

1 Horizontal
Horizontal integration means that two firms join up making the same product *at the same stage of production*. Back in Unit 1 (Section 1.2) we looked at the different stages of production involved in the manufacture of a table: cut down the tree, make the table from the wood, sell the finished article. An example of horizontal integration would be if two firms of lumberjacks joined together, two table manufacturers, or two furniture retailers.

2 Vertical
Vertical integration involves the joining of two firms making the same product *at different stages of production*. So the table manufacturer may join up with the firm of lumberjacks, or the manufacturer and the retailer may join together. Fig. 6.14 shows the difference between the two.

Mergers

When two firms of any size or type join together this is called a **merger**. There are several reasons why they may wish to do this:

- to increase their market share and power;
- to benefit from economies of scale (provide a better product or service at a cheaper price; increase production, etc.);
- to increase sales and profits.

There may be undesirable aspects to this, however – particularly from the point of view of consumers:

- The merged firm may gain a **monopoly** in the market – meaning there is no effective competition – and may use this to charge higher prices and provide a poorer quality service.
- There may be diseconomies of scale if the merged firm is too large.
- People inside the firms to be merged may use their position to carry out 'insider trading' on the Stock

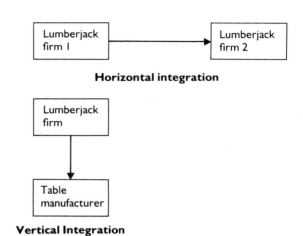

Horizontal integration

Vertical Integration

Fig. 6.14   Examples of integration

Exchange whereby they buy up their shares now in the knowledge that the price will rise further after the merger *which only they know about at the moment.*

Also, some members of the firms involved may not want the merger:

- Some may lose their jobs in the resulting re-organisation – particularly members of the smaller firm.
- Some may lose their positions of authority – again mainly members of the smaller firm – and become 'smaller fish in a larger pond'.
- In general many people do not like, and are afraid of, *change* – the principle of **inertia**.

The Monopolies and Mergers Commission

This body was set up originally in 1948 precisely because of the dangers involved in mergers. Its structure has changed over the years and it now has the power to investigate any merger that is referred to it by the **Office of Fair Trading**. It can investigate a merger when the merged company would either:

(a) have 25 per cent or more of the market;
(b) have assets of more than £15 million.

The job of the Commission is to decide whether any proposed merger is likely to act 'in the public interest' and the onus is on the companies that wish to merge to prove that it will. Of course, the whole idea of 'the public interest' is very vague – is it more important that the resulting product should be cheap or of good quality; or is it more important still that as many jobs as possible should be retained? Thus the findings of the Commission will really represent only a point of view.

EXERCISE

Read the following article carefully and answer the questions that follow.

The main reason for the confusion of merger policy in the UK stems from the wide definition of the public interest – the philosophy which is supposed to be the basis on which decisions are made.

Section 84 of the 1973 Fair Trading Act gives the Monopolies Commission considerable freedom to determine the public interest. However, it does contain guidance about five specific areas which should be taken into account. These are: competition; the interests of consumers; costs and innovation; a balanced distribution of industry and employment to the UK; and exports.

But the Commission can also take into account 'any other matter which it considers in the particular circumstances to be relevant'.

This wide-ranging freedom means that it is difficult for companies to know what factors the Commission will actually take into account. Other competition laws, such as the restrictive practices legislation, have a narrower set of guidelines. However, these also have been criticised for enabling companies more easily to find loopholes.

In many other industrialised countries merger controls tend to be based more firmly on competition issues, such as whether or not a merger would create a monopoly situation which would harm the public.

In the UK, some form of merger control has existed since 1965, but the present procedures, involving the Office of Fair Trading, as well as the Commission, date from 1973.

There is a five-stage process for merger control:

1   All mergers which involve assets of more than £15m or which would give the merger company more than 25 per cent of the market are considered by an OFT mergers panel for possible referral to the Commission.

In 1981 the panel considered some 164 mergers (involving total assets of almost £44bn) and referred eight to the Commission. In the first 10 months of last year, some 138 mergers were looked at and 10 – a record number – were referred.

2   The actual referral advice is made by the Director-General of Fair Trading to the Trade Secretary, who can accept or reject it. Since 1973, the Trade Secretary has overruled the Director-General only on a handful of occasions.

3   The Commission has some six months to weigh up the public interest issues involved and reach a conclusion. The investigation is carried out by six or seven commissioners.

4   The Director-General also offers his advice on the Commission's report to the Trade Secretary.

5   The Trade Secretary then has to decide whether to accept the Commission's conclusions. He can enforce the decision with statutory powers.

In the 18 years of merger investigations, 20 mergers have been abandoned once referred, while 22 have been found to be against the public interest after an investigation. Some 25 mergers were found not against the public interest and thus allowed to proceed.

1   The article gives five 'guidelines' that the Commission is supposed to take into account when deciding 'the public interest'. List them with a short explanation by each as to what it means and what its importance is for British industry.

2   Why is it difficult for firms to know what the Commission will *actually* take into account?

3   How does the practice in other countries differ from that in the United Kingdom?

4   Explain, in your own words, the 'five-stage process for merger control'.

6.8 Transport

The method chosen to transport raw materials and finished goods round the country will depend, largely, on the type of product in question.

Road transport

This is the most popular form of transport for industry; about 60 per cent of inland freight is carried by road, usually in huge container lorries. There are several reasons why road transport is considered to be the most convenient form:

- The goods can be carried 'door to door' – they do not need to be collected from a main-line station depot.
- Lorries can travel at any time that they wish and are not dependent on timetables.
- Lorry transport is economical, particularly because of competition among road haulage contractors.

However, road transport is not suitable for some very heavy loads and is subject to delays caused by road works or heavy traffic. In addition there are a number of **social costs** associated with road traffic that do not apply to other forms of transport.

Fig. 6.16

Fig. 6.15

Railway transport

Some people would argue that far more goods should be carried on the railway. It would have some of the problems that road transport avoids, i.e. it still needs transporting from the station and is subject to a timetable. On the other hand, it avoids traffic and road works and reduces the social costs involved in road transport. However, there are greater **capital costs** involved in rail traffic – the cost of the equipment, lines, trains, maintenance, etc.

FOR DISCUSSION

Explain what a social cost is. (Look back to Unit 1, Section 1.5, if you need a reminder.) When you have worked it out, decide what might be the social costs that are associated with freight being carried around by road. How do these compare with the social costs involved in rail transport?

Inland waterways

In the eighteenth century, the canal network extended across much of England and Wales. However, it is a slow form of transport, and during the late nineteenth and early twentieth centuries many of the canals were left to deteriorate until they became unusable (unnavigable).

Fig. 6.17

Despite the advantages of no traffic jams, no noise, pollution or high overheads, the inland waterways in the United Kingdom are restricted in their commercial use, although some – for example, the River Trent Navigation, River Weaver Navigation, South Yorkshire Navigation, and the Caledonian Canal in Scotland, which all link with the sea – transport bulk commodities such as coal and chemicals. Other countries, notably Germany, make greater commercial use of their inland waterways.

Today, the canals are being cleaned up and reopened, mainly for recreational and holiday traffic. Almost 24,000 boats are now licensed to use the waterways, the highest ever. More than four million tons of freight was handled in the year ending March 1988.

Sea transport

As you would expect this is mainly for conducting trade with other countries, although some goods are carried round the United Kingdom by sea – notably from London to Newcastle-upon-Tyne via the North Sea. Trade is mainly carried out by **cargo liners** which operate on a regular route to a fixed timetable and they usually carry a few passengers. Goods are also carried on **tramp** ships. As the name suggests they have no fixed timetable or route but will carry cargo anywhere.

Fig. 6.18

Air transport

Aeroplanes are the fastest form of transport, which is particularly significant for perishable goods and when the goods have to be carried over long distances. It is an expensive form of transport, however; airports are not very widely distributed across countries, leading to the necessity for arrangements to take the goods to their intended destination, and it is not economic for short distances.

Fig. 6.19

EXERCISE

In each of the following cases suggest the most suitable means of transport, taking all the factors mentioned into account and explain your choice fully:

(a) a collection of records from Birmingham to London (remember that records are very fragile);
(b) a box of oranges from New Zealand;
(c) a consignment of oil from Saudi Arabia;
(d) a delivery of meat from Yorkshire to Glasgow;
(e) a consignment of coal from the Midlands to London. (Coal stocks are high so there will be no particular hurry for the delivery.)

6.9 Distribution

In Section 6.8 we looked at the ways in which goods are carried around the country. There are, however, a number of people or firms through whom the goods are 'passed' and these are known as **channels of distribution.**

Fig. 6.20

The most usual route is shown in Fig. 6.20. The product is *made* by a **manufacturer**, then sent to a **wholesaler** who stores it, usually in large warehouses. Wholesalers have the advantage of having large amounts of storage space that the manufacturer may not have, but they charge money for their services, of course. This is the 'middleman's cut' which pushes up the price to the consumer. The **retailer** buys from the wholesaler and sells to the customer. Anywhere that you can go and buy goods is known as a **retail outlet.**

Fig. 6.21

Not all goods follow this path, however. The wholesaler may sell direct to the consumer, missing out the retailer (Fig. 6.21). A well-known example of this is the cash-and-carry store where huge quantities of food and supplies are held in enormous warehouses and the customer buys directly. It is necessary to have a special member's card to use these stores, however – not anybody can just 'walk in'.

Fig. 6.22

They are usually used by small stores, restaurants and hotels to whom the stores sell at a discount in return for the customers buying 'in bulk'. Alternatively, the manufacturer may sell straight to the retailer, missing out the wholesaler (Fig. 6.22).

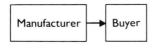

Fig. 6.23

Finally, both the retailer and the wholesaler may be missed out, when the manufacturer sells straight to the customer (Fig. 6.23). Perhaps the most common example of this is a craft centre, where the craftsman or craftswoman produces goods for sale. They tend to make only small quantities so storage is not a problem and it is easier and cheaper to sell straight to the consumer.

How Marks & Spencer organise their distribution

Marks & Spencer is a Public Limited Company with 264 stores in the United Kingdom and ten stores in Europe, Canada and the USA. They buy goods – mainly clothing and food, although they have diversified into other areas such as furniture – directly from the manufacturer and made to their own specifications, keeping a close check on quality control and price.

As their range of merchandise widens there is a need for increased sales area. The capacity of outside warehouses has grown from just under 750,000 sq. ft. to nearly 4 million sq. ft. over a period of just ten years. Their warehouses fall into three main groups:

1 local warehouses run by stores;

2 large warehouses, controlled by Marks & Spencer's head office, each of which services several large stores;

3 large warehouses, operated by contractors and working for a group of Marks & Spencer stores 24 hours a day. A typical unit holds £30 million of stock and covers an area three times the size of a football field. In 1987 £4 billion worth of merchandise was delivered to Marks & Spencer stores by 1,000 vehicles which operate from regional depots set up for the company by specialist distribution companies. Delivering food is a particular problem because its freshness must be maintained. The temperature is held at a constant level and the delivery is rejected if the temperature should rise at any point during the journey between the supplier and the store.

EXERCISE

Write down what you would expect the usual channel of distribution to be for each of the following products, and then research to find out what actually happens:

(a) a hand-crafted chair;
(b) a record;
(c) a television set;
(d) a Welsh dresser;
(e) a drill;
(f) eggs.

6.10 The marketing mix

So far we have looked at elements of marketing separately. If a product is to be successfully marketed, however, the different elements must be combined in the correct **mix.** Let us go back to Jean and Ron's restaurant and consider how they can combine all the elements that we have looked at – and one or two that we have not – to produce a successful service.

Fig. 6.24 shows the main elements of the marketing mix.

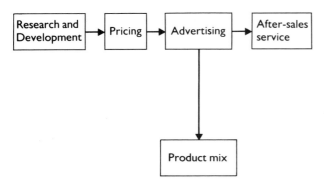

Fig. 6.24

Research and Development

Before they could cook anything it was necessary for Jean and Ron to look carefully into what food they could provide and the best methods of cooking it. In the same way the Research and Development Department in a factory investigates the possible products that could be made and the best, most efficient ways of producing them. In a 'high tech' industry such as electronics or computing 'R & D' is extremely important as new developments and improvements are being made all the time and companies need to keep up with them. In a restaurant, on the other hand, this element would play a less important part in the mix – unless they were planning to invent their own recipes constantly; they are more likely to concentrate on what is already known.

Pricing

As we have already seen it is very important for any business to price its goods correctly. A restaurant will probably have a lot of competition from other places and so it will be particularly important to 'get the price right'. However, a 'high tech' firm producing specialist equipment is likely to have more of a 'monopoly of knowledge' and so pricing may be less important.

Advertising

As we have already seen in Section 6.3, advertising is particularly important for a restaurant, which may face heavy competition, but will be less so for a 'high tech' firm in a specialist field.

Related to advertising is the **product mix** which looks at the different types of product made by one firm and how they relate to each other, particularly in the eyes of the customers. This can be seen clearly in the case of a restaurant: the way in which different types of food are offered on the menu and the combinations in which they are presented will be crucial to the restaurant's success.

After-sales service

This is an aspect that we have not yet looked at. It refers to the need to provide a service to customers *after* the product or service has been sold. For instance, Marks & Spencer have a high reputation as a **retailer** (seller) for providing excellent after-sales service: any article considered unsuitable or unsatisfactory by the customer can be quickly and easily exchanged either for money or for another article.

A firm that provides specialist equipment would need to be closely involved in after-sales service; for example, a computer hardware firm will expect to install the equipment on the customer's premises after purchase and provide back-up advice and electronic/engineering expertise during the equipment's life. For a restaurant, on the other hand, such a service is not necessary; hopefully the customers will leave the restaurant satisfied with both the quality of the meal and the service they have received, and this will encourage them to return.

EXERCISE

For each of the businesses listed below, put the elements of the marketing mix in the order of priority that you would expect for them. Explain your choice each time. N.B. You are only taking an 'educated guess' and even the element that you put on the bottom for any of them might still be important for the business. (If you really cannot decide between two elements you can put them on the same level.)

(a) the manufacturer of a new type of chocolate;
(b) a sauna;
(c) a pet shop;
(d) a machine-tool manufacturer;
(e) a garage;
(f) a cabinet maker.

6.11 Other elements of marketing

Branding

This is an idea that follows on from the discussion about advertising. We saw in Section 6.3 that one of the main aims of advertising any product is to give it a distinct identity from other similar products and so make it seem more desirable. This is called creating a **brand loyalty**; creating a 'name' that people will identify with and buy – even possibly at a higher price than similar goods sold under another name. An obvious example is Heinz Baked Beans. Such a successful advertising campaign has taken place over the years that many people now identify baked beans with Heinz; even though there are many other types of beans on the market, none of them sell as well as Heinz even though few people would seriously claim that there is much difference in quality. They have been particularly successful in capturing the children's **segment** (part) of the market.

EXERCISE

Divide into groups and decide on a name for your cushions that you think will create maximum brand loyalty. Present a short talk to the rest of the class explaining the thinking behind your choice. Which segment of the market are you aiming for?

Packaging

This is considered very important in creating the right *image* for the product. For instance, cosmetics may be packaged in soft, pastel colours to appeal to a woman's femininity, while DIY tools like drills and screwdrivers are sold in practical packs using 'manly' sombre colours or bright, 'no-nonsense' primary colours to suggest a rugged, straightforward approach. Perhaps part of the secret is in trying to persuade people that the image the product suggests will *make* them into that sort of person.

> ### FOR DISCUSSION
> 1 Look at the three examples of packaging shown in Fig. 6.25. Take each in turn and describe the sort of people that you think the manufacturers are aiming at.
> 2 How important a part of packaging do you consider 'the ideal image' plays? If each of the products shown were packaged in brown paper instead, would that reduce their appeal in your eyes? Discuss your opinions with the class.

Fig. 6.25   Examples of packaging

Promotion

This could be said to be a mixture of advertising and packaging – with a bit of branding thrown in! When you go into a department store there must be occasions when you see a special stall for a particular product with, quite possibly, a **demonstrator** explaining how the product works and trying to persuade people that it is worth buying. This is particularly common with new products that firms are trying to get established on the market. This is known as **promotion** and differs from advertising in that it tends to take place at the 'point of sale'.

Pricing

A very important decision to be made is what price a firm should charge when it introduces a new product or service. We saw that Jean and Ron were so keen to 'get it right' that in their questionnaire they included a question on the sort of price that customers would be prepared to pay. A firm should bear several factors in mind when deciding what price it should charge:

- The firm will *usually* wish to cover its costs of production to ensure that it does not make a loss – and hopefully that it makes a profit.
- It needs to charge a price that will attract custom. There is no point in charging such a high price that no one is prepared to buy the goods. This could conflict with the first consideration.
- If a product is entering the market for the first time or if there are a number of firms in competition, the firm may be prepared to charge a price that is *lower* than the cost of production to help it 'penetrate' the market. This is known as a **loss leader** and obviously the firm hopes that this will only be temporary and that the

product will soon be established in the market and able to take a higher price.

- Sometimes a firm will sell a product at a loss indefinitely and **subsidise** it from the profits of other goods in that product range.
- The extent of competition from other firms in the same market will influence the price that can be charged. If there are a number of firms producing a similar article the scope for charging a high price is far less than if the firm is the sole supplier – when it has a monopoly.

EXERCISE

A firm producing a particular article has the following costs to pay 'per unit' produced:

Wages £1.00
Raw materials £1.00
Power 50p
General Expenses 50p
'Allocated' fixed costs £1.00

(a) If the firm decides that it wishes to make a 10 per cent profit on each article produced, what price would it charge?
(b) Ten per cent is quite a low profit margin. Explain all the various reasons why the firm might be prepared to accept this.
(c) Using the same figures calculate the price that would produce a 50 per cent profit margin and explain the sort of market that would allow this to the firm.

The exercise gives examples of what is known as **cost–plus** pricing; we are calculating the **mark up** on the cost price.

6.12 Marketing success: Derwent Valley Foods

Consett is a small town in Durham. In 1982 the steel works, which had employed a large proportion of the adult males, closed down as part of the general contraction of the British steel industry. This created a high level of unemployment and also left a lot of disused land and machinery where the closed steel works had been.

In March 1982 Derwent Valley Foods Limited was formed in Consett by a team of four directors, three of whom came from another food company that was situated locally. They noticed that there was no 'snack food' for adults, and that this represented an 'unexploited niche' in the market. So they decided to manufacture a high-quality, high-priced, innovative product to appeal to that market.

British Steel Corporation helped them with a loan and provided disused premises for their use until they could use their present premises. They still work closely together.

The inspiration for the brand was found in the film *Around the World in Eighty Days*. The main character in the film was called **Phileas Fogg,** which became the **brand name** for the **product range.** Different countries inspired the products themselves, and the initial range consisted of four products: Tortilla Chips; Californian Corn Chips; Mignons Morceaux; Shanghai Nuts.

The Phileas Fogg brand broke the 'usual' rules of advertising in a number of ways:

- The products did not attempt to appeal to 'the majority' but tried to build up a strong, loyal following from a minority of the public.
- The company insisted upon natural flavours. This surprised their suppliers because they were three times the price of the artificial flavours that other manufacturers used.
- The packaging did not have a 'window' through which the product could be seen despite the fact that consumers had said in market research that they wanted to see the product. All other snack foods have one.
- The packaging was unusual and expensive. It promoted a long shelf-life – necessary in the delicatessen trade.
- The retail price of the product is much higher than that of most other bag snacks.
- The name was difficult to say and most consumers did not associate it with the film, so there seemed to be little reason for it apart from 'whimsy' on the part of the manufacturers.

Phileas Fogg Does it Again!

PRESERVATIVES • NATURAL FLAVOURS • NO PRESERVATIVES • NATURAL FLAV

PHILEAS FOGG FINE FOODS FROM AROUND THE WORLD

PUNJAB PURI

Spicy golden crackers lightly seasoned with traditional Indian spices.

- ✳ Unique addition to The Best Selling Adult Snack Range
- ✳ Authentic Indian Texture and Spices
- ✳ Available in Two Sizes — 100 g Standard — 40 g Snack

Fig. 6.26

The current product range has the four original products plus Java Crackers and Punjab Puri (see Fig. 6.26). (You might like to consider who the company hoped to appeal to with their latest launch.)

In 1986 Derwent Valley Foods was appointed joint winner of the 1986 **Business Enterprise Award.** The purpose of the award is to 'recognise and publicise the contribution made by business enterprise to British society through the creation of wealth and employment'. The main sponsor of this award is the **Confederation of British Industry** (CBI). There is also a panel of judges under the guidance of Britain's oldest business school, the Henley Management College. Other sponsors include Barclays and Lloyds Banks.

The workforce rose from 16 in 1982 to 165 in 1987. In the same period the total factory size in square feet expanded from 12,500 to 50,000. The product is widely distributed by both small and large grocers and is now sold in sixteen countries. In a few years the company believes that it has achieved two main things:

1 It has highlighted the fact that there is always a market for innovation and quality despite the presence of big companies.
2 It has helped to create a new environment of experimentation and prosperity in the depressed north-east of England.

EXERCISE

Write an essay on the origins and development of Derwent Valley Foods. Try to include the following points:

(a) under what circumstances they were set up;
(b) what type of market they aimed to appeal to – how was this shown in their product range and their brand name?
(c) how they broke the usual rules of marketing;
(d) how their success can be seen in terms of their growth and the recognition that they have gained;
(e) what they think they have achieved and what this shows for other people.
(f) Research the range's popularity among your family and friends. What do they think of the brand name, packaging, flavours, variety available?

Fig. 6.27

CASE STUDY:

6.13 The Fruity Bar

Choco Ltd, the chocolate manufacturers, were having a lean time. The public appeared to be getting fed up with their leading brands so they decided that new ideas were needed. The Managing Director turned to his leading managers:

'We need a new line and we need it quickly. John, I want the Research and Development Department to think of a new type of chocolate bar – not too many new ingredients but a new arrangement that will appear to be different. The Production team must be geared up to producing it quickly and the Marketing boys must prepare the market research to ensure that the right product is being made for the consumers and for packaging, promoting and advertising the product to get it sold.'

The Research and Development Department came up with a chocolate bar that was full of different types of dried fruit. This was a variation on the sort of chocolate products that they had produced so far but fitting in with current trends towards more healthy eating. There were one or two imperfections in the early bars – but the technical problems were soon ironed out. The Marketing Department prepared a survey on people's chocolate eating habits and also arranged for **test sampling** in selected high streets. There was a lot of discussion about the name of the bar – Fruitcake, Chocofruit and the Raisinbar were 'thrown about' until *Fruity Bar* was finally agreed. Packaging was also fully discussed. The argument revolved around those who believed that packaging was not particularly important in determining people's buying decisions so money should be saved by having relatively plain packaging and those who claimed that a bright, eye-catching package increased sales and so was a worthwhile investment.

Advertising was obviously extremely important in introducing the new line into the market. £10,000 was made available for this.

Sales grew extremely slowly in the first six months. The Managing Director was becoming very worried and talked about pulling out of this line 'before it loses any more money'. He was dissuaded by the Marketing Director: 'Look, Charles, you know as well as I do that products are usually slow in getting off the ground. We have a winning formula – I know it. Just give me a few more months – and think about how much money we would lose if we pulled out now.'

It looked at first as if the Marketing Director was going to have to eat his words – and possibly lose his job. Sales did not pick up for the next four months; then they suddenly took off and, for the next year, the Production Department could hardly keep up with the demand. Retail outlets which had never stocked their goods before put in orders. Production workers were put on to compulsory overtime. It could not last, though, and after a few months of rocketing sales the rate of increase began to slacken off.

The Marketing Manager thought of many strategies to try to increase sales again – but to no avail. Soon sales were falling. The Managing Director was not too bothered. They had had an excellent year during which they had made a lot of money and already the Research and Development Department had other plans and the money that *Fruity Bar* had made was very useful in financing their research . . .

Appendix

The total cost of launching *Fruity Bar* was £100,000. The running costs were £15,000 per month. The sales figures were as shown in Fig. 6.28.

Fig. 6.28   Fruity Bar sales

Month	Sales (£'s)
1	5,000
2	5,000
3	6,000
4	6,000
5	6,000
6	7,000
7	8,000
8	6,000
9	9,000
10	15,000
11	25,000
12	45,000
13	60,000
14	80,000
15	90,000
16	90,000
17	60,000
18	50,000
19	30,000
20	20,000
21	10,000
22	5,000

QUESTIONS

1   Explain in your own words the roles of: (a) the Research and Development Department; (b) the Production Department; (c) the Marketing Department. (6)

2   Why was market research necessary 'to ensure that the right product is being made for the consumers' and how will packaging, promotion and advertising help to sell the product? (Explain them separately.) (5)

3 What was the thinking behind the production of a chocolate bar with dried fruit? (3)
4 What is test sampling and why do firms carry it out? (3)
5 Which side would you have taken in the discussion over packaging? Explain your answer. (5)
6 Can you think of a better name than *Fruity Bar*? (2)
7 Suggest some appropriate advertising media for their campaign. Which would you recommend? (5)
8 Draw a product life cycle for *Fruity Bar*. Indicate the marketing strategies that would be appropriate for each phase. (8)

9 Draw up a questionnaire that you think would be appropriate to test the viability of this product. (10)
10 Using the figures given in the Appendix calculate:
   (a) the number of months that it took *Fruity Bar* to pay back the initial investment; (5)
   (a) the loss made during the first six months; (5)
   (c) the profit made at the end. (3)

   _____
   (60)

7.1 Planned and market economies

One thing that our friend Dai Jones did not understand was the difference between the way in which business was run in a country like the United Kingdom and the way in which it was run in the Soviet Union. He knew that they were different but he was not sure in what way. Jim, a friend who lectured in politics at the local college, explained it to him one evening.

Dai: As far as I can see it's simple. In this country people can do what they like, while in the Soviet Union they have to do what the government tells them. Is that it?

Jim: Well, it's not quite as simple as that. The Soviet Union and a number of other countries in Eastern Europe such as Hungary, Bulgaria and Rumania have what is called a **planned economy**.

Dai: What does that mean, then? What exactly is 'planned'?

Jim: The whole economy – at least, in theory. As you have found yourself, in this country you can set up your own business if you can find a market and raise the money. You buy in the raw materials and employ the labour that you need. If you make a profit you survive; if you don't you close down. In other words, you operate in a **market economy.** The government is not involved.

Dai: The VAT man wants his share and there are all those rules about safety at work, advertising, equal opportunities and all that sort of thing. Then I have to pay rates, corporation tax, seek planning permission if I want to expand my factory . . .

Jim: Yes, that's quite true. Even in a market economy, where firms only survive if they satisfy a need that people are prepared to pay for, the government do intervene to raise money for public spending, ensure that safety standards are followed and that consumers are not misled by advertising and that people are not discriminated against because of their sex or race. They also help some businesses with loans and grants for various reasons.

Dai: So how is this different from a planned economy?

Jim: Well, in a country with a planned economy, the government actually owns and runs most of the businesses.

Dai: Like nationalised industries in this country?

Jim: That's right – except that about 10 per cent of our industries are owned by the government while very little is *not* owned by the government in those countries.

Dai: How does a planned economy work?

Jim: All economic activity is controlled by a committee which is in turn controlled by the government – in the Soviet Union it is called **Gosplan.** This committee, to put it simply, decides *what* will be produced in each industry, in what *quantities* and the *price* at which it will be sold. The committee also puts forward a plan of production which individual factories then attempt to meet.

Dai: Doesn't this mean that the government will have to tell people what job they can do – otherwise they may not have enough workers in the right place to fulfil their plan?

Fig. 7.1(A)   Living conditions in eastern Europe – a planned economy

Fig. 7.1(B) A Market economy

Jim: Exactly. It also reduces the choice of goods that are available to consumers. You have to buy what the state factories produce. This, plus the pressure to meet the production targets, can mean that the quality of goods produced is very low. If you buy a pair of shoes in Russia the chances are that they will fall apart after a few months.

Dai: Surely there must be some advantages in having a planned economy or no country would have one.

Jim: Oh, there are. With a 'national plan' the government can ensure that investment is put into areas that are 'useful' rather than those which happen to produce a large profit. The Soviet Union managed to build up its industry in just ten years, between 1928 and 1938, while it took this country over half a century to make similar gains in industrial production.

Dai: Didn't this involve a lot of people being killed?

Jim: It did, but that is not necessarily the result of the economic system. It could be said to be the leaders, particularly Stalin, but that is not what we are discussing. Anyway, the market economies tended to use child labour in industrialisation which the Soviet Union never did. The other benefits today of having a planned economy are that it is possible to plan to use up all the available labour force,

i.e. eliminate unemployment. This does mean that some people are doing jobs of pretty doubtful value, however, and this is called 'disguised unemployment' but it does avoid the indignities of the dole queue. With controlled prices people can also be spared inflation – although it is generally accepted now that higher prices in some areas may be necessary to improve the quality of production and resource allocation in general. It should also be possible, within a planned economy, to have less difference in income between different people.

Dai: Aren't there some changes going on in the Soviet Union at the moment – **perestroika** or something?

Jim: Yes – but we haven't time to go into them tonight . . .

EXERCISE

1   From the conversation between Jim and Dai, pick out all the things that you think are wrong with the way that our economy is run at the moment and explain how a planned economy tries to avoid these drawbacks.

2   Do you think the methods used in a planned economy solve a country's economic problems in a satisfactory way for all concerned? What disadvantages can you find?

3   Explain exactly, in your own words, how a planned economy differs from a market economy.

4   Divide your page into two. Head one side 'Advantages of a planned economy' and the other 'Advantages of a market economy'. Do the same on the next page with the 'Disadvantages' of each and enter in the correct column the points that you can pick out of the dialogue – plus any more that you can think of.

EXTENSION ACTIVITY

Right at the end of the dialogue Dai mentioned **perestroika** which is the Russian word for the economic changes that are taking place there at the time of writing. Research to discover exactly what this term means and the changes in the economy that it is intended to bring about and *why* it was felt to be necessary. You can consult your teacher, your parents and you can look up back issues of newspapers in the library (1987 and 1988 would be the years to concentrate upon). Write up your findings either in the form of a report or an essay.

7.2 Inflation

Dai asked Jim to explain about **inflation,** which he found rather confusing: the government had stated that inflation was falling yet the prices of building materials and also of food and household goods still seemed to be rising.

Jim: You understand that inflation is a situation of rising prices. It also means that the value of money is falling; a given amount of money will buy – or is *worth* – fewer goods.

Dai: Yes, I know that. What I don't understand is what causes it, how it can be stopped and exactly how it affects my business activities.

Jim: Prices usually rise for one of three reasons. It may be that *costs of production* are rising – wages, raw materials, rent, the rate of interest on loans, or profits. If that happens we have **cost push inflation.**

Dai: So if my workers ask for a wage increase and I grant it but then increase my prices to compensate, I have caused cost push inflation.

Jim: Right – or if you decide that you want more profit and raise prices to produce it. You are an **entrepreneur** and your services are a 'factor of production' in the same way that those of labour are.

Dai: What is the second way?

Jim: If *demand* for goods and services rises in the economy this will *pull* their prices up and so you will have **demand pull inflation.**

Dai: Is that like an auction where the price will continue rising as long as people are bidding for it, but if there aren't many bidders it will go for a low price just to make sure that it is sold?

Jim: Exactly. The third way is one that we have heard a lot about from the present government.

Dai: Is that something to do with the 'money supply'?

Jim: Yes. As you probably know, the Bank of England, on behalf of the government, issues notes and coins that we spend. If the supply of those notes and coins rises too quickly – more quickly than the ability of the economy to produce goods for them to buy – then the excess money will push prices up.

Dai: Isn't that rather similar to the 'demand pull' theory?

Jim: It is not totally different, except that it is saying that the 'excess demand' only has one possible source – the money supply. With 'demand pull' there could be lots of causes.

Dai: I suppose that if the government reduces taxes that would increase demand because people would have more money to spend.

Jim: Exactly. You're getting good at this!

Dai: So what can the government do about all this?

Jim: You tell me. For instance, what if they think that inflation is caused by high costs of production?

Dai: Well, they will want to reduce those costs. They would try to keep wage increases down and forbid excess profits. Raw materials may be more difficult because they are often bought from abroad.

Jim: It's called a **prices and incomes policy.** Such policies were used quite a lot in the 1970s but rather fell out of favour because they were difficult to enforce – the unions didn't want restrictions on their collective bargaining powers. Incidentally, there is something that can be done about raw material prices, but I will tell you about that some other night. What about 'demand pull'?

Dai: Keep demand for goods and services down, I suppose. If reducing taxes increases demand as I said before, the government could increase the taxes to reduce demand. Raising interest rates would keep borrowing down and so reduce credit sales – washing machines, furniture, cars, etc. Keeping wages down would also help.

Jim: All this is called **fiscal policy** – influencing the economy by altering how much the government raises and spends. Incidentally, you have forgotten that the government could reduce its own spending; for example, if they build a school they put money in people's pockets as wages.

Dai: The money supply problem is easy – just print less money!

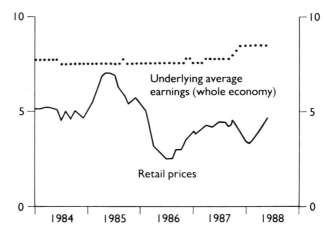

% changes on a year earlier

Fig. 7.2   Retail prices and average earnings 1984–88

Jim: Yes, it sounds easy. The present government tried it but actually found it very difficult in practice. The factors that make up the demand for money are very complex and the money supply kept on rising whatever they did. In the end they gave up the attempt. Meanwhile a number of firms were forced out of business and unemployment rose sharply. As firms got into difficulties they borrowed more to try to keep afloat – it is called **distress borrowing** – and this pushed the money supply up further.

Dai: Nevertheless, inflation *has* fallen. Why is that?

Jim: There are a number of factors. High unemployment has kept wage demands – and demand for goods and services – low and they have kept raw material prices down in a way that I will explain on another occasion.

Dai: You promised to explain to me the effect that inflation has on business.

Jim: Oh, yes. Haven't you found that if you sign a contract to build a house at a certain price you lose out if the price of materials rises in the meantime?

Dai: Yes, I have, now you come to mention it.

Jim: This is a problem for anyone who works on long-term projects. Rising prices increase demands from workers for higher wages. This does not affect firms that just sell in this country so much, because if everyone's prices are rising then nobody suffers.

Dai: But if firms are trying to sell goods abroad where prices may not have been rising so quickly they may be priced out of the market.

Jim: You really are getting good at this!

EXERCISE

Write a short essay on inflation. Make sure that you include the following points:

(a) a good definition of inflation;
(b) an explanation of the three different causes of inflation;
(c) an explanation of the remedies that are available;
(d) an explanation of the effects on business of inflation.

EXTENSION ACTIVITY

Carry out some research into the different inflation rates in the United Kingdom over the last ten years and the policies that were used at different times to deal with it. You should find the information in economic journals in the library. Write up your findings in the form of a report with graphs where appropriate.

7.3 Exchange rates

Jim had promised Dai that he would tell him how governments could affect the prices of goods coming in from abroad (see Section 7.2). First, he needed to explain a little about **exchange rates**.

THE POUND TODAY			
$1.774		**Dm3.2269**	
Trade-weighted average 97.3		Sweden	9p 11.0775
Australia	48¾p 2.0570	Switzerland	36¼p 2.7523
Austria	4½p 22.68	U.S.A.	56¼p 1.7740
Belgium	1½p 67.65	**TOURIST RATES**	
Canada	47p 2.1208		
Denmark	8p 12.4650	Austrian schilling	22.25
France	9p 11.0058	French franc	10.83
Germany	31p 3.2269	German mark	3.175
Holland	27½p 3.6450	Greek drachma	268.00
Hong Kong	7¼p 13.8922	Italian lira	2330.00
Ireland	83p 1.2045	Maltese lira	0.578
Italy (100)	4¼p 2367.00	Portuguese escudo	259.00
Japan (10)	4½p 223.96	Spanish peseta	199.50
Norway	8½p 11.8100	Swiss franc	2.705
South Africa	23¼p 4.2445	U.S. dollar	1.7850
Spain	½p 204.00	Yugoslavian dinar	8800.0

Fig. 7.3 Exchange rates

Jim: If you go to Spain on holiday you don't take pounds and pence with you, do you?
Dai: No, I go to the bank and exchange pounds for pesetas.
Jim: I'll bet that you look at the exchange rate between pounds and pesetas to see how many you are going to get, don't you?
Dai: You bet!
Jim: Well, you are looking at the **rate of exchange** between one currency and another. In just the same way, a firm that is **exporting** (selling) goods to America or is **importing** (buying) goods from America looks at the rate of exchange of dollars for pounds.
Dai: I don't follow.
Jim: If we are exporting goods to America the Americans know that dollars are no use to us so they exchange dollars for pounds; similarly if we are importing goods from them we exchange pounds for dollars because pounds are no use to them and the rate of exchange will partly determine the price at which the goods are traded.
Dai: Can you give me an example of that?
Jim: OK. Imagine that the exchange rate of the two currencies is £1 equals $2. A British firm selling £1,000 worth of goods to America will charge the Americans $2,000.
Dai: I'm with you so far.

Jim: What if the exchange rate changes so that £1 equals $1.50 – how much will the goods cost in America now?
Dai: $1,500.
Jim: Yes. The pound has been **devalued** – it's worth fewer dollars than it was before. This makes British goods cheaper abroad and so should encourage more to be sold.
Dai: So if the pound is worth more dollars – say £1 equals $3 – British goods will be more expensive abroad and that same £1,000 worth of goods will now cost $3,000 and so should reduce demand for them.
Jim: That is called **revaluation**.
Dai: This does not explain how the government manages to keep down the price of raw materials that they import as you told me last night.
Jim: Let us go back to the original exchange rate – £1 equals $2. So $2,000 worth of American goods . . .
Dai: . . . will sell for £1,000 in Britain.
Jim: That's right. How much will the same goods cost in Britain if the exchange rate falls to £1 equals $1.50?
Dai: Um . . .
Jim: Well, under the same exchange rate £2 equals $3, so the ratio is 3 to 2 or 3 dollars to 2 pounds, so the price in pounds must be two-thirds of the price in dollars . . .
Dai: Two-thirds of $2,000 is £1,332.
Jim: So the devaluation of the pound has forced the price of imports up. This means either that we buy less or – as is the case with Britain which tends to import essential goods such as raw materials and food – prices and therefore *inflation* will rise. So if the government wishes to reduce inflation . . .
Dai: It will revalue the pound because that will make imports cheaper.
Jim: For instance . . .
Dai: . . . If the exchange rate rises to £1 equals $3, then 2,000 dollars of American goods will cost . . .
Jim: . . . £666. The problem with this, as can be seen in Britain over the last few years, is that it also makes exports more expensive which can cause unemployment because firms cannot sell their goods abroad.

Summary

- The rate of exchange refers to the amount of one currency that can be bought with another.
- When countries trade with each other they buy and sell currency. The country that is buying goods – the **importer** – will buy the currency of the country that is selling the goods – the **exporter** – in order to pay them for the goods.
- If the value of a currency falls, i.e. it is **devalued,** the exports of that country become cheaper and its imports become more expensive.
- So a devaluation makes it easier for a country to export but may cause inflation if it does not reduce its imports.

- If the value of a currency rises, i.e. it is **revalued,** the exports of that country become more expensive and its imports become cheaper.
- So a revaluation reduces inflation but can cause unemployment as exporters cannot sell their goods and so are driven out of business.

EXERCISE

1 Explain why countries buy each other's currencies.
2 Explain the effects of a devaluation on the price of exports and imports. What effects will this have on business and the economy?
3 Repeat question **2** for a revaluation.
4 Imagine the exchange rate is £1 = $4. If a British firm wishes to sell £3,000 worth of goods to America what will be the dollar price?
5 How much will those same goods cost if the pound is: (a) devalued to £1 = $3.50; (b) revalued to £1 = $4.25?
6 Repeat questions **4** and **5** for a British firm buying $10,000 worth of goods from America.

7.4 Trade

Put at its simplest 'trade' means to exchange. So if I decide to get rid of my old car by selling it to a garage who give me a new one in exchange (they will probably want some more money as well), I am said to have **traded** it. This sort of activity is carried on all the time within a country. When we talk about 'trade' we usually mean **foreign trade,** however; in other words, the exchange of goods *between different countries.*

It would be possible – although difficult – for most countries to make and grow enough items for them to survive without trade. This is known as **autarky** (self-sufficiency) and an example of a country that tried it was China during the 1950s and 1960s. There are two big disadvantages for countries following that path, however:

1 The choice of goods available is going to be severely restricted.
2 It may be extremely expensive for them to produce certain necessities.

To give an example of that last point, imagine that Great Britain decided to stop trading. We could manage to produce many manufactured goods, although they would be more expensive than many that we could buy abroad – compare the prices of British and Japanese hi-fi equipment. We could grow quite a lot of our own food. What about fruit like bananas and oranges? They need a warm climate which we do not have. Now we could build enormous greenhouses all over the country, but imagine the cost both in terms of money – **financial** – and the land given up that could have been otherwise used – **opportunity.** The only advantage of not trading is that of national 'independence' and an absence of reliance on other countries and changing exchange rates. If you look at the disadvantages, though, you soon see why most countries engage in some trade – even China, who is now actively looking for it.

If a country sells goods abroad it is said to **export** goods. If it buys goods from abroad it is said to **import** them. A country **buys** 'foreign exchange' – the currencies of other countries – in order to pay for imports and *sells* it in order that it might export. Among the different types of goods that are traded are the following:

- **Visible**
  As the name implies these are goods that can be 'seen'; they are physical goods, e.g. machines, cars, food, etc.
- **Invisible**
  These cannot be 'seen'. They are services of various types, such as banking, insurance, tourism, etc.

This leads to the different **accounts** by which the trading position of a country is measured:

Fig. 7.4   Different types of trade

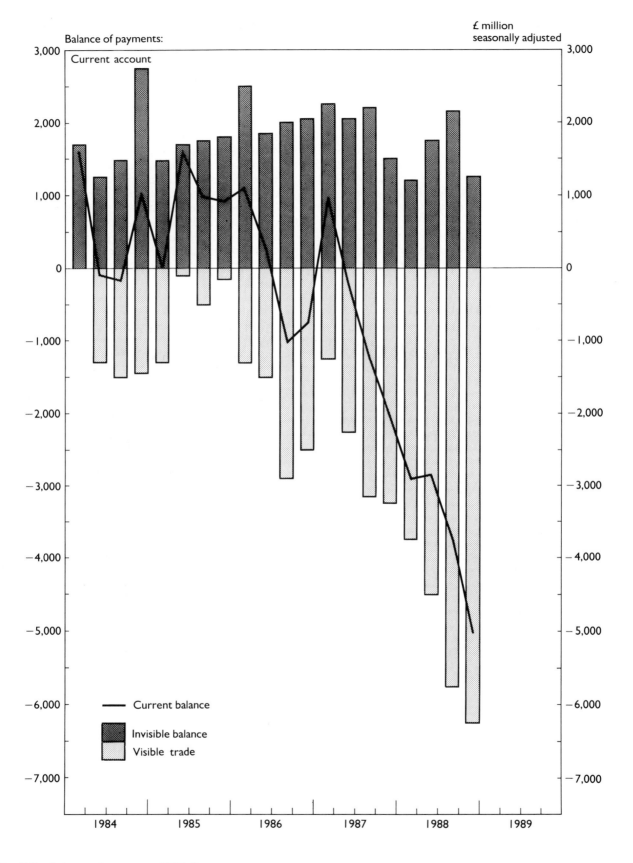

Fig. 7.5   Balance of payments 1984–9

- **The balance of trade**
  Balance of Trade = Visible Exports − Visible Imports.
  So if a country exports £75 million worth of goods and imports £60 million its balance of trade is equal to a **surplus** of £15 million.
- **The balance of payments on current account**
  (Balance of Payments on Current Account = (Visible + Invisible Exports) − (Visible + Invisible Imports))
  So if the country referred to above exported services worth £25 million and imported services worth £50 million:

$$\text{Balance of payments} = (75 + 25) - (60 + 50)$$
$$= 100 - 110$$
$$= -10 \text{ million}$$

i.e. a **deficit** of £10 million.

So a surplus occurs when exports exceed imports and more money enters the country than leaves it. A deficit occurs when imports exceed exports and more money leaves the country than enters it.

Dealing with a deficit

It is generally considered to be a good thing to have a surplus, although it must always be remembered that 'one country's surplus is another country's deficit' and excessive surpluses are generally discouraged. A small deficit can usually be easily covered with reserves of foreign exchange. A large deficit is generally a cause for concern, however. It can be tackled in one of the following ways:

- **Encourage an increase in exports**
  This is not an easy thing for governments to do. They can give grants and loans to exporters. The **Export Credits Guarantee Department** of the Department of Trade also provides insurance against non-payment of debts by customers. The direct help that they can provide is limited, however. Firms will only export if they can provide the right product at the right price at the right time.
- **Restrict imports**
  This is far more within the power of a government. They can place direct physical restrictions, e.g. by imposing **quotas** on imports, or they can 'tax' imports, by means of **tariffs;** these can either be specific – a fixed amount, or *ad valorem* ('according to value') – a percentage of the value of the imports. They can impose **exchange controls** which reduce the availability of foreign currency, or they can **subsidise** domestically produced goods to make them cheaper in relation to those from other countries.

There is the danger that other countries will **retaliate,** thus removing the point of the exercise by restricting your own exports. That is a danger with any type of import restriction. Nevertheless, many countries think it necessary, not only to correct a deficit on their balance of payments but also to protect their industry against competition that is sometimes considered 'unfair' – particularly from countries that can sell their goods cheaply because they pay their workers very low wages. Such competition can result in job losses at home if domestic industries cannot sell their goods because of imports.

EXERCISE

Study the graph in Fig. 7.5 and answer the following questions:
1 Explain, in your own words, the difference between the invisible balance, the visible trade and the current balance.
2 As you can see, there are four 'readings' every year; in other words, one every **quarter**. What was the:

(a) invisible balance in the second quarter of 1984;
(b) visible trade in the fourth quarter of 1987;
(c) current balance in the first quarter of 1985?

Try to read off your answers as accurately as possible.
3 When was the current balance in greatest deficit? Explain all the policy options open to the Government and state the problems associated with each. Which would you recommend and why? (You will need to refer to Section 7.3 on exchange rates.)
4 Take the readings for the invisible balance and redraw them as a **line graph** (as the current balance has been drawn).

7.5 Taxation

Everything was going well for Build-Anything Ltd, but one thing continually annoyed Dai – government interference. The fact that he was charged VAT meant that he in turn had to charge prices that were 15 per cent higher than they would otherwise be; Dai had to pay income tax on all his personal earnings; the firm had to pay 'crippling' rates to the local authority; there were many safety regulations that the government insisted that he operate on his building sites. He could not advertise exactly as he wished and there was always some 'consumers' body' ready to jump down his throat if the firm made the slightest mistake. Of course, there had been a very generous grant provided by the government when he decided to open a new branch just outside Liverpool . . .

So why do governments levy taxes and make rules and regulations? Is it just to make life difficult for businesses? Jim, the college lecturer who had helped Dai understand several economic points, explained.

Jim: It's like this, see. Governments have to raise money from us so that they can spend it on us.
Dai: Well, that doesn't make a lot of sense. Why bother in the first place?
Jim: Would you build a road, or a school, or a hospital, or give a grant to a firm with the money that you now pay in tax?
Dai: I suppose not. But I wouldn't have enough, would I?
Jim: Precisely. So the government 'brings together' everybody's money and spends it on things that we all need. It has two main types of tax to raise money – **direct** and **indirect**.

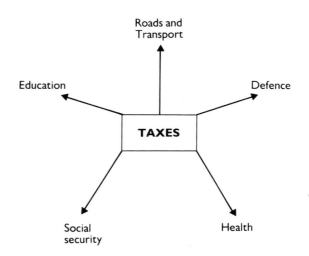

Fig. 7.6 **Where our taxes go**

Dai: What's the difference?
Jim: Direct taxes are levied 'directly' on your income.
Dai: You mean income tax?
Jim: Right. There are other direct taxes – corporation tax on company profits, capital gains tax on profits from increases in capital values, death duties on inheritances and capital transfer tax on expensive 'gifts' of capital assets.
Dai: What about indirect taxes?
Jim: Those are the ones that you really moan about – principally VAT, which stands for Value Added Tax. They are taxes not on *income* but on *spending*.
Dai: Why is it called 'value added tax'?
Jim: This is because there are several stages in the movement of a product from the producer to the consumer. The forester chops down the tree, sells the wood to the furniture manufacturer who makes the table, and so on. Each stage of production adds to the value of the product and the finished table is worth far more than a piece of untreated wood. At each stage of production the seller pays VAT but only on the difference between what they have bought the product for and what they have sold it for. In other words, on the *value added*.
Dai: That tax really adds to my costs.
Jim: Yes, but you pass it on to your customers in the price that you charge, don't you? The problem is that the higher VAT is the more prices will rise of the goods and services that we all buy – in other words it adds to *inflation*.
Dai: I suppose that in some ways direct taxes are fairer than indirect taxes.
Jim: Why do you say that?
Dai: Well, you pay more income tax; for example, if you earn more – isn't the word **progressive**? While you pay the same VAT whatever you earn – and poorer people tend to spend a higher proportion of their income than richer people. That's a **regressive** tax, isn't it?

Jim: That's right, although some people would argue that it is fairer that people should have low income tax so that they can keep their money and choose whether to spend it or not. If they pay high VAT it is their choice because they have chosen to spend their money rather than save it.

Dai: There's no doubt that high taxation of whatever type is bad for business; high VAT raises prices and reduces demand, high income tax reduces the incentive to work. Why should I bother if all my earnings are going to be taken away in taxes?

Jim: Yes, but who would be the first to complain if the government grants to industry were reduced, or the roads in the area were not maintained, or schools were closed down, or if hospitals and medical services were reduced? . . .

EXERCISE

1 Explain why governments levy taxes.
2 Name three things that governments spend money on.
3 Explain the difference between direct and indirect taxation and give an example of each.
4 Why is Value Added Tax so called?
5 Why does VAT add to inflation – but not to Dai's costs?
6 Explain the difference between a progressive tax and a regressive tax.
7 Opinion is divided as to which is fairer – progressive or regressive tax. Explain both arguments.
8 Why does Dai think that high taxes are bad for business? Distinguish between direct taxation and indirect taxation in your answer.
9 What advantages for business does Jim find from the money raised in taxation?
10 Do you think that it is more important to keep prices down and encourage people to work hard or to provide services and grants? Explain your answer.

EXTENSION ACTIVITY

Write to your local taxation office asking for information leaflets and research in the library to find out about as many different types of tax as you can. Make a note of their purpose, whether they are direct or indirect and whether they are progressive or regressive. With each note explain what effect you think that a change in the tax would have on business activity – if any.

7.6 The European Community

The map in Fig. 7.7 shows the twelve present members of the European Community (EC). It was formed when six of the countries signed the **Treaty of Rome** in 1957. Great Britain did not join until 1972 after two previous applications to join had been turned down. The EC is also known as the **Common Market** and, as the name implies, the idea is that the member countries should all trade together in one market. This has several advantages for the members:

■ They are moving towards a system of freedom of trade between the members – no tariffs or quotas.
■ There is a **common external tariff** for all the members on goods imported from outside the Community; in other words, any goods imported from outside are taxed at the same rate by all.
■ Firms established in one member country may work in any other.
■ Any citizen of a member country may work in any other EC country without a work permit or any other restriction – 'free movement of labour'.

The EC has detailed policies in a number of areas that need to be briefly looked at.

Regional policy

Just as unemployment is higher in certain regions of the United Kingdom than others so that is the case for all EC countries. Consequently, there is a **Regional Fund** and also a **Social Fund** to provide help which is seen as being 'economically worth while'. All member states contribute to these funds and the general aim is to reduce inequality and bring about a more even distribution of wealth.

The Common Agricultural Policy (CAP)

This is an aspect of the EC that has attracted a lot of publicity – and much of it unfavourable. Its aim is to provide a secure income for the farmers who produce food and to encourage the Community to be self-sufficient in food and to reduce imports. Briefly, the Commission of the EC set a **target price** for food products – the price that they would expect it to receive. Imported foods are also set at a certain price which does not 'undercut' EC farmers. (One reason that was given by opponents of British entry was that we would no longer be able to

Fig. 7.7   **The twelve members of the European Economic Community**

Fig. 7.8   EEC trade headquarters in Brussels

obtain cheap food from the Commonwealth countries –
particularly Australia and New Zealand.) If they do not
reach this price then a **levy** is placed on them. Of course, if
the price rises above the price of imports the levy is
abolished and refunds provided. If the target price is not
reached farmers may sell off their stock to **Intervention
Boards** who will give them the full price and then keep the
product off the market to try to force prices back up
towards the target price.

    You should be able to see clearly the advantages and
disadvantages of this system. It provides *stable prices* and a
steady income for farmers but at the expense of *higher
prices* than may be necessary and possible *shortages* on
the market. Many people associate the CAP with 'butter
mountains' and 'wine lakes' – produce that was
deliberately held back from sale and left to waste to
maintain food prices at the level that the Community
deemed necessary.

Trade policy

This is very important for understanding what the EC is
about. As already stated, they are moving towards a
system of 'free trade' among member states and a
common external tariff with countries outside the EC. This
has the advantage of providing all the member states with
an opportunity to compete in each other's countries.
Unfortunately it has not worked out particularly well for
the United Kingdom; because many of the other
economies in the Community have been stronger than
ours, we have *imported* more goods from EC countries
than we have *exported* to them.

EXERCISE

1   Explain, in your own words, why the EC has a
    regional policy.
2   Explain how the Common Agricultural Policy works
    and what its advantages and disadvantages are.
3   What is the 'trade policy' of the Community and why
    has it not worked out well for the United Kingdom?

<hr>

EXTENSION ACTIVITY

The year 1992 will be very significant for the EC.
Carry out some research to find out why. You
could write up your findings in the form of a
newspaper article.

7.7 Population and the economy

Fig. 7.9 Different economies

Compare the following stories about the population of two different countries.

'Gothland has a population of 60 million people. The average size of family is 2.3 children and the average life expectancy is 71 years. Everyone stays at school until they are at least 16 years of age and so the population is well educated which means that all jobs in a modern technological society can be filled. It also means that people live longer, as medical knowledge and sanitary conditions are improving all the time; the economy is strong enough to support the increasing numbers of elderly people that this produces, however. The population's basic needs are satisfied, on the whole, and so there is a market for high-quality, luxury goods.'

'Lapvia has a population of 23 million people. The average size of family is 7.6 children and the average life expectancy is 40 years. Education stops at 8 years for most children so the majority are qualified to do only unskilled jobs. This has greatly hampered the development of industry in the country which is mainly made up of subsistence farming. Medical knowledge and sanitary conditions are poor which keeps life expectancy short. As most of the population does not have its basic needs satisfied there is only a market for basic necessary goods.'

Key terms
- **Average size of family**
  The average number of children in a family is worked out by taking the total number of children and dividing it by the total number of families.

- **Average life expectancy**
  The average age that an inhabitant of a country is expected to live to is calculated by looking at the age at which inhabitants die and dividing the total by the number of people in the survey.
- **Modern technological society**
  The 'advanced' economies that live mainly by the produce of machine-dominated industry.
- **Subsistence farming**
  The less developed countries live mainly by the produce of farming in which people tend just to produce enough for their own needs with little left over to trade – no *surplus*.

POINTS FOR DISCUSSION
Compare the population of the two countries in terms of: (a) average size of family; (b) average time spent at school; (c) average life expectancy. Discuss the effect that the differences in these areas will have on the type of business in each country.

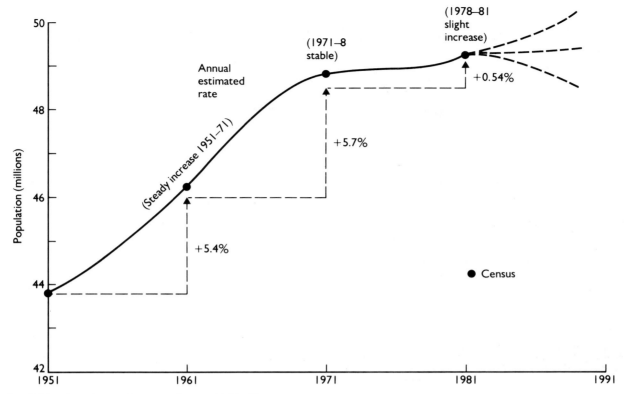

Fig. 7.10   Population change in Britain 1951–81

EXERCISE

The United Kingdom Population
Study the graph in Fig. 7.10 and answer the questions that follow.

1 Read off the population figures for 1951, 1961, 1971 and 1981 as accurately as possible. Try to account for the percentage changes given.
2 Why do you think that the rate of population growth fell off during the 1970's (think about changing attitudes towards abortion, contraception and working women).
3 Think of two reasons why industry might regret the lack of population growth in the 1970's.
4 What is the link between the figures for the 1970's and redundancies for teachers?

EXERCISE

Study the figures in Fig. 7.11 and answer the questions that follow.

1 Discuss the difference in meaning between 'size of total working population' and 'size of employed population'.

Fig. 7.11   The working population

2 Give some reasons for the increase in both figures between the two years.
3 Why have more females entered the labour market in 1986?
4 How would you account for the difference between the total of males plus females and the total employed population?
5 Display all the given information on one *bar graph*.
6 Calculate the levels of unemployment in 1983 and 1986 and add these to the graph.

Manufacturing v. Services

The simplest way to divide the different types of jobs is between manufacturing and services. **Manufacturing** involves the making of physical goods – machine tools, refrigerators, furniture, etc. **Services** provide the other things that people need, and also help manufacturing industry – banking, insurance, education, health, etc.

Numbers employed in manufacturing and services

	1981	1986
Manufacturing	6,109,000	5,361,000
Services	13,093,000	13,854,000

	1983	1986
Size of total working population	26,163,000	27,229,000
Size of employed population	23,191,000	24,030,000
Male/Female breakdown	Male 11,692,000	11,681,000
	Female 8,945,000	9,392,000

Thus in five years 748,000 jobs were lost in manufacturing and 761,000 jobs were gained in services. Let us take examples of both types of industry:

- The *coal* industry has lost 100,000 jobs since 1981 and 110,000 jobs have gone in *mechanical engineering*.
- The *Health Service*, on the other hand, has gained 110,000 jobs while *banking and insurance* has gained 130,000 jobs.

EXTENSION ACTIVITY

Carry out some research into the question 'Why have we been losing jobs in manufacturing and gaining them in services? What has been the result of this?' Your History teacher may be able to help as well as your Business Studies teacher. The library will also have information. Write up your findings in the form of a report.

EXERCISE

The graph in Fig. 7.12 shows the number of people employed in manufacturing between 1984 and 1987, with the *predicted* figures for 1988. The year is divided into **quarters.** Take the figure for the *first* quarter of each year and draw a **bar chart** showing the decline in manufacturing employment.

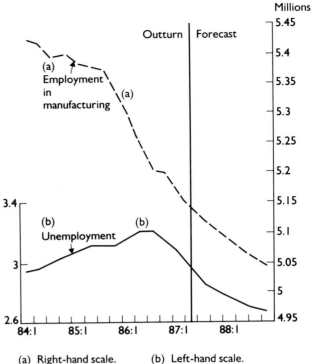

(a) Right-hand scale.   (b) Left-hand scale.

Fig. 7.12   Employment in manufacturing, and unemployment

7.8 The Stock Exchange

Everybody has heard of the Stock Exchange but not many people really understand how it works. This section will attempt to explain.

History

This can be traced back to the sixteenth century. At that time British merchants and seamen were trying to expand their trade overseas, often in little known parts of the world such as the Far East. It was sometimes difficult for them to raise money, however, and so they began to form **joint stock companies.** These were really the first limited companies because the merchants invited people to put money into the venture in return for a share of the profits if successful while accepting the risks of failure. The 'shares' could be traded, enabling investors to convert their holding back into cash when required.

If the shares in these companies were to be bought and sold it was necessary to have a 'market' where this could take place. Originally this was in coffee shops around the City of London but in 1773 the dealers moved into the first building called the Stock Exchange. It played an increasingly important role in the nineteenth century as new firms were founded during the Industrial Revolution. Many of them depended on the Stock Exchange to provide a market in which they could raise their finance.

In 1908 the official distinction between **brokers** and **jobbers** was introduced. Brokers traded in shares on behalf of their clients, while jobbers operated in the market on their own account and did not deal with the public directly. You had to be one or the other to be allowed on the floor of the Stock Exchange. Members of the public may only watch the trading from the Visitors' Gallery.

The 'Big Bang'

The distinction between jobbers and brokers remained until 1986 – the year of the 'Big Bang' which made great changes in the way that dealing was carried out. These can be summarised as follows:

■ No more jobbers and brokers. Firms on the Stock Exchange are now simply **broker dealers** who can either represent clients or buy and sell shares on their own behalf. Some of them are called **market makers** who will buy and sell certain types of shares regularly.
■ No more **minimum commission.** Previously there was a minimum fee set by the Stock Exchange that all brokers had to charge for their services. Now all fees are negotiable between the client and the firm.
■ No more restrictions on outside membership of member firms. Previously they had to be controlled by individual members. Now outside institutions could become **corporate members.**

■ No more recording of share dealings and prices on paper. The information technology revolution has reached the Stock Exchange. The new system, called **Stock Exchange Automated Quotations (SEAQ)** enables information about share prices to be displayed on screen from anywhere in the world within minutes of them being formed.

Why were these changes introduced?

There were two main reasons for these changes:

1 It became obvious that London firms were small in comparison with those from other countries and when 'exchange controls' were abolished in 1979 the smaller British broking firms did not do well when competing for business with the larger foreign firms.
2 The government believed that the minimum commission, the restrictions on membership of the Exchange and the broker/jobber distinction were all acting against competition. The Office of Fair Trading took the Stock Exchange to the Restrictive Practices Court. The changes avoided a long, expensive and damaging court case by meeting many of the objections of the government. Most members of the Stock Exchange believed that changes were overdue.

EXERCISE

How share buying works
Look carefully at Fig. 7.14.

1 What are the *two* institutions that an investor can ask to buy shares for him or her in a company? How does this differ from the system before 'Big Bang'?
2 What does the broker/dealer look for on the SEAQ screen?

Fig. 7.13   Stock Market dealing room

HOW SHARE BUYING WORKS:

THE INDIVIDUAL INVESTOR

[1] An INVESTOR deciding to buy some shares in a company can:

(a) Contact a member firm of The Stock Exchange (A BROKER/DEALER)

(b) Ask a bank to act for them. (The bank would anyway buy the shares via a BROKER/DEALER.)

[2] The BROKER/DEALER consults a SEAQ screen. SEAQ is the Stock Exchange Automated Quotation system, on which MARKET-MAKERS display their buying and selling prices to all the users of the system simultaneously. The prices are shown in pence per share.

SEAQ
SHARE PRICE INFORMATION

[3] There are always at least two MARKET-MAKERS competing to quote prices for the shares of any company, and for the most active shares there can be as many as twenty competing for the business of the investing public.

The MARKET-MAKER quoting the highest price for buying the shares, or the lowest price for selling, is at the top of the SEAQ screen, so the broker can see which market-maker is offering the best price for the deal that the INVESTOR wants to make.

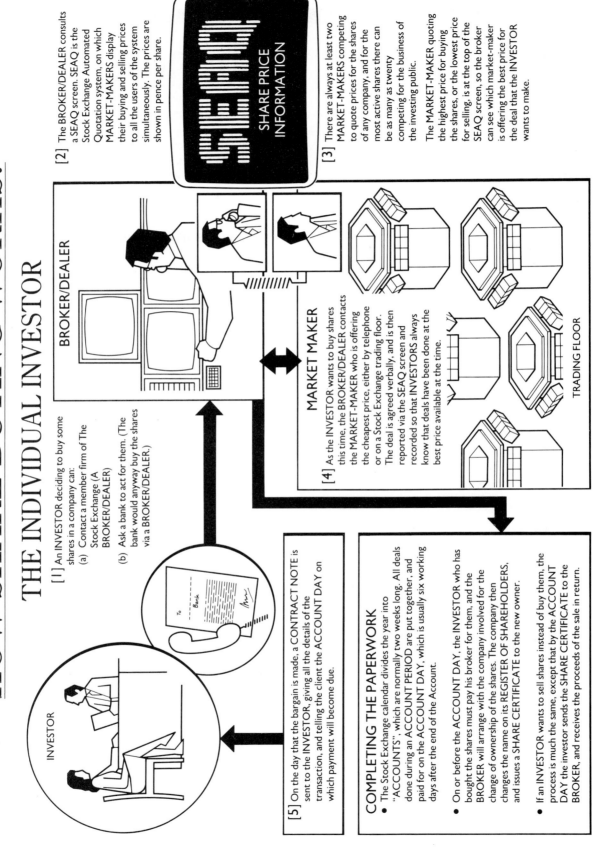

BROKER/DEALER

MARKET MAKER

[4] As the INVESTOR wants to buy shares this time, the BROKER/DEALER contacts the MARKET-MAKER who is offering the cheapest price, either by telephone or on a Stock Exchange trading floor. The deal is agreed verbally, and is then reported via the SEAQ screen and recorded so that INVESTORS always know that deals have been done at the best price available at the time.

TRADING FLOOR

INVESTOR

[5] On the day that the bargain is made, a CONTRACT NOTE is sent to the INVESTOR, giving all the details of the transaction, and telling the client the ACCOUNT DAY on which payment will become due.

COMPLETING THE PAPERWORK

- The Stock Exchange calendar divides the year into "ACCOUNTS", which are normally two weeks long. All deals done during an ACCOUNT PERIOD are put together, and paid for on the ACCOUNT DAY, which is usually six working days after the end of the Account.

- On or before the ACCOUNT DAY, the INVESTOR who has bought the shares must pay his broker for them, and the BROKER will arrange with the company involved for the change of ownership of the shares. The company then changes the name on its REGISTER OF SHAREHOLDERS, and issues a SHARE CERTIFICATE to the new owner.

- If an INVESTOR wants to sell shares instead of buy them, the process is much the same, except that by the ACCOUNT DAY the investor sends the SHARE CERTIFICATE to the BROKER, and receives the proceeds of the sale in return.

Fig. 7.14   How share buying works

3 How does the broker/dealer use the screen to find the best deal for the client?
4 How does the broker/dealer contact the market maker who is offering the lowest price? How is any deal reported?
5 What is the **contract note** and when does it appear?
6 What is the proof of your ownership of shares?

EXERCISE

Imagine that, instead of wanting to buy shares you wish to *sell* them. Explain in your own words exactly what processes you would go through (using Fig. 7.14 for reference if you need to). Illustrate your answer if you think that it will help.

Do we need a Stock Exchange?

Some people would argue that the Stock Exchange is unnecessary, together with the enormous salaries that many who work on it can earn. They would claim that there is a cheaper way of exchanging shares, or that we should have a 'planned economy' in which investment funds are directed by the state (see Section 7.1). The present method, they believe, is a waste of resources and channels money that could be invested in industry – which earns wealth – into the 'financial sector' which does not. As long as we have a market economy there must be a market for shares in public limited companies because this is the only way in which those companies can raise capital and people will always want to buy and sell their shares. Whether the elaborate and expensive system that now exists is necessary is much more debatable.

FOR DISCUSSION
Discuss the advantages and disadvantages of having a Stock Exchange and consider if there are any 'cheaper' ways of buying and selling shares.

EXTENSION ACTIVITY
Write to the Stock Exchange and ask them for details about the difference in the way it operated before 'Big Bang' and how it operates now. You could write a project entitled 'The Stock Exchange: Before and After'.

7.9 Business activity in the UK economy

The term 'economy' that you hear about so much on the television, radio and in the newspapers – the **media** – simply refers to the way in which a country is able to feed its people and provide them with the other goods and services that they want; in other words, how a country 'earns its living'.

As we have already seen in Unit 2, the economy of the United Kingdom is a **mixed economy.** This means that ownership of businesses is a 'mixture' of private and public: some are owned by private individuals (sole traders and partnerships), some are owned by shareholders (private and public limited companies) – these are all in the **private sector.** Others are owned by the government – these are in the **public sector.** There have always been far more firms in the private sector in the United Kingdom and, at the time of writing, the balance is being tipped further that way with the Conservative government's **privatisation** programme (see Unit 2, Section 2.5).

All businesses exist to provide the goods and services that people want and are prepared to buy. The value of goods and services produced is called the **Gross Domestic Product (GDP).** In 1985 it was measured to be £305.8 billion; the United Kingdom has the world's sixth largest GDP after the USA, Japan, the USSR, West Germany and France. In terms of the rate of **growth** of GDP – the amount by which it rises each year – we are faring worse than most other Western industrialised countries and we are eighteenth in the table for GDP *per head* (the amount for each member of the population), just above Libya.

One thing that has improved our growth rate during the years 1977–87 has been the discovery of **North Sea oil.** This also helped our Balance of Payments (see Section 7.4) because we were able to import less oil from other countries and at the same time export our own oil. Production started falling after 1986, though, and the oil is expected to run out by the early–mid-1990s.

EXERCISE

1 The table in Fig. 7.15 shows the 'main sectors' of economic activity in the United Kingdom. The 'value added' column shows the amount that each sector added to the value of GDP in billions of pounds.
   (a) Take each 'sector' in turn and explain, in your own words, what it produces. (Ask your teacher about any sectors you are not sure of.)
   (b) Apart from Manufacturing, which sectors had the highest value added?
   (c) You will see that one of those sectors in the previous answer employs far more people than the other. Think about what each sector produces and explain why this might be the case.
   (d) What effect would you expect the introduction of more advanced equipment in all sectors to have on employment? Explain your answer.
   (e) Draw two **pie charts** to show the information in both columns graphically.
2 The table in Fig. 7.16 shows the ten largest companies in the United Kingdom.
   (a) All but one of the companies named are now privately owned. Which is the exception?
   (b) Three were previously in the public sector and one was half owned by the government. Name the four and research to find out *when* they were privatised.
   (c) Eight of the companies are in the **energy** sector. Which are the two exceptions?
   (d) As you can see from the table in Fig. 7.15, energy has been the fastest growing sector. Why do you think that this has been the case?
   (e) Which was the second fastest growing sector? Which account on the Balance of Payments will this benefit?

Fig. 7.15   Main sectors of economic activity

	Value added £bn (1984)	Employ-ees '000 (Dec. 1985)*	Volume change in output % pa (1975-84)	% share of gdp at current factor cost (1984)
Agriculture, forestry, fishing	6.0	332	3.0	2.1
Energy and water supply	31.5	583	7.7	11.3
Manufacturing	68.4	5,433	–1.1	24.4
Construction	15.8	935	–0.7	5.7
Distribution, hotels and catering	37.0	4,491	0.4	13.2
Transport and communications	19.8	1,266	1.3	7.1
Financial services	37.0	1,881	5.7	13.2
Ownership of dwellings	16.7	108	1.6	6.0
Education and health	25.7	2,885	2.0	9.2
Public administration	18.9	1,536	0.1	6.7
Other services	18.2	1,670	2.9	6.5
Adjustment and residual	–15.1	—	—	–5.4
Gdp at factor cost	279.9	21,122	1.3	100.0

*Figures are for Great Britain. The other columns in the table are for UK as a whole.

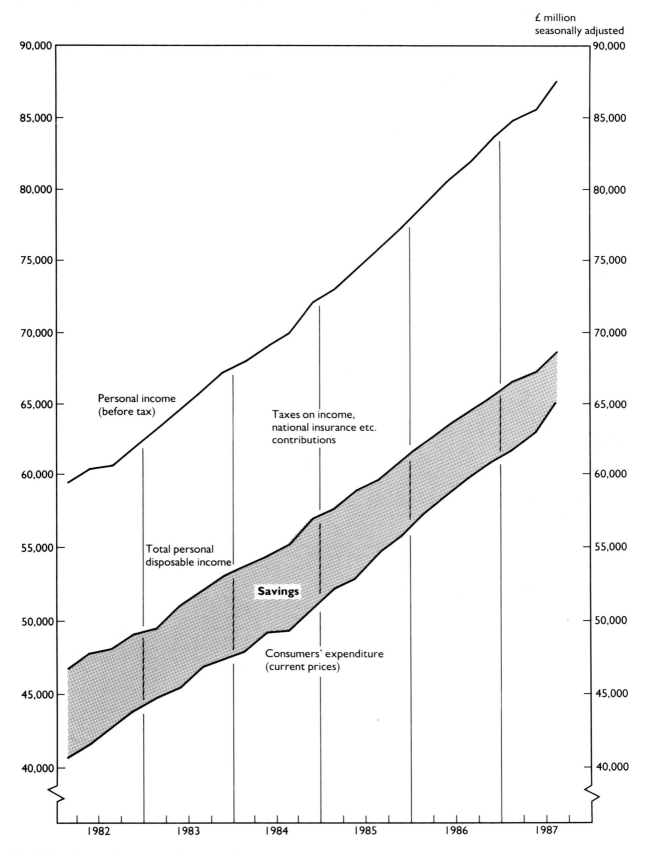

Fig. 7.18   Personal income and consumption

Fig. 7.16 The largest UK enterprises

	Turnover £bn	Employees '000
British Petroleum	44.1	130
Shell Transport and Trading	29.5	n/a
BAT Industries	14.4	213
Imperial Chemical Industries	9.9	116
Shell UK	9.6	17
*British National Oil Corporation	9.6	n/a
*Electricity Council	9.6	140
Esso UK	7.6	7
British Telecom	6.9	245
*British Gas Corporation	6.4	97

*Public corporation or nationalised industry.

Government expenditure

Of course governments spend money also. Some of it is raised in taxes (see Section 7.5); some is borrowed from the public in exchange for **gilt-edged securities** – bonds that earn their holders a rate of interest. The amount by which the government spends more than it raises is called the **Public Sector Borrowing Requirement (PSBR)**. Fig. 7.17 shows exactly *what* the government spends money on.

EXERCISE

1 Write a sentence or two explaining exactly what each of the items listed in Fig. 7.17 are.
2 Why do you think that social security payments account for such a large portion of government spending?
3 Why is it necessary that items like Education and Defence should be provided by the government? Why could it not be left to private firms?
4 Show the information in the table in the form of a **bar graph.**

Consumption expenditure

We can also look at the amount of money that **consumers** spend on goods and services. The graph (Fig. 7.18) shows **gross earnings** (personal income before tax), **total personal disposable income** (money left to spend after income tax and national insurance have been taken off) and **consumers' expenditure.** The difference between the last two is obviously **savings.** As you can see all rose steadily between 1982 and 1987.

The pie chart (Fig. 7.19) shows the proportion of income spent on different types of goods and services during 1986.

Fig. 7.17 Analysis of general government expenditure by function

	Total expenditure % share	As % of gdp at market prices
Social security benefits	29.0	13.3
Education	11.7	5.3
Defence	11.6	5.3
National health service	11.5	5.3
Debt interest	10.7	4.9
Housing and amenities	4.9	2.3
General public services	4.3	2.0
Public order and safety	4.0	1.8
Transport and communication	2.4	1.1
Mining, manufacturing and construction	1.7	0.8
Agriculture, forestry and fishing	1.5	0.7
Recreation and cultural affairs	1.4	0.6
Fuel and energy	0.9	0.4
Other expenditure	4.4	2.0

EXERCISE

Convert the information contained in the pie chart (Fig. 7.19) into a **bar chart.** Do you think that these figures are true for *your* family? You could ask your parents to calculate how much of their income they spend on each of these – if they don't object to telling you!

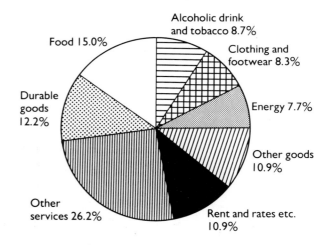

Fig. 7.19 Share of consumers' expenditure 1986 1980 prices

7.10 Interest rates

The cost of borrowing money is the rate of interest. If you lend £5 to a friend of yours you are unlikely to ask for interest – just the re-payment of £5 unless you are a particularly ruthless business-person! In the business world, however, interest on loans is required. Much larger sums are involved than with personal loans and there are financial institutions that earn their money through the interest charged on loans – notably banks and building societies.

There are two main 'economic' reasons for charging interest on loans:

1 to act as a reward for the risk taken that the money will not be re-paid, i.e. that the borrower will **default;**
2 to act as an incentive for people to lend their money rather than spend it, i.e. a reward for **foregone consumption.**

In most economies the rate of interest acts as the measure of the **opportunity cost** of capital projects. The opportunity cost is the 'foregone alternative'; in other words, if the government decides to build a road it *could have* spent the money on many other things – a school, a hospital, a subsidy to a firm – all of these represent the opportunity cost of the road. For the purpose of accounting, however, it is assumed that they would have invested the money spent on the road. Thus the expected return on the road must exceed the rate of interest if the project is to be considered economically worth while. This is also known as the **discount rate.**

The process by which the interest rate is set is quite complicated. It is based on the rate that the **Bank of England** charges as the 'lender of last resort' to the

discount houses, which buy and sell short-term government bills. If they run short of funds they borrow from the Bank of England and the rate that they are charged tends to set the pattern for the rest of the economy – the banks, building societies, etc. It is important to remember that there is not just one interest rate in the economy but many; for instance, the interest rate charged by a bank for a personal loan is far less than the rate charged by credit card companies such as Access and Visa. It is becoming increasingly common for large stores to offer 'interest free credit' on sales of **consumer durables** (goods that will last a long time and are expensive, e.g. fridges, washing machines, cookers, furniture suites, etc.), on condition that the loan is re-paid within a certain period of time (often ten months).

The interest rate is extremely important to business for a number of reasons:

- Firms often need to borrow money to invest in new equipment so that they can expand. The higher the rate of interest the more expensive will that be for them, i.e. the **financial cost** will be high.
- A higher rate of interest will make it more expensive for firms to finance existing debt.
- A high rate of interest will make investing in industry less attractive in relation to saving the money or buying an interest yielding bond. People will not risk putting the money into industry which may fail – while a bond will always pay interest – unless the *profit* that they expect to earn from industry is much greater than the *interest* that they know they could earn from saving. In other words, a high interest rate raises the opportunity cost of investing in industry.

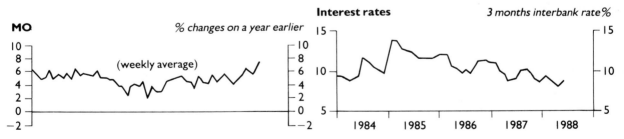

Fig. 7.20   Interest rates 1984–88

CASE STUDY:

7.11 Tax, inflation and rates

The conversation that he had with Jim convinced Dai that he needed an economist to advise him on the state of affairs in the economy and how it would affect his company, Build-Anything Ltd. At great cost he secured the services of Mel McWhizzo, a leading financial expert. Jim had taught Dai that taxes, inflation, interest rates and exchange rates were all important to him, so Mel's first job was to draw up a report on the state of the economy at the moment, what he predicted it would be the following year and how, if at all, Build-Anything Ltd would be affected.

'Over the last few years the trend has been to shift the burden of taxation from direct to indirect taxes. When the present government came to power in 1979 the rate of income tax was 33 per cent while the rate of VAT was 8 per cent. One of their first acts was to reduce income tax to 30 per cent and increase VAT to 15 per cent. Income tax is now 25 per cent in the pound. The government has also extended the range of goods that charge VAT to include such items as take-away foods.

'Inflation has fallen substantially. During the mid-1970s it rose to 25 per cent per annum. By 1979 it had fallen to 9.8 per cent. Since then it has fallen further and now it is hovering around the 5 per cent mark. The policies used by the government to achieve this have changed somewhat over the years, however. The prospect is for a small rise in inflation over the next year or so – possibly to 6 or 7 per cent. Nothing very dramatic is likely to happen, however.

'Interest rates have gone up and down. They always do. Recently, the trend has definitely been upwards. The main reason for this is that the government wanted to attract foreign money into the country to make up for the Balance of Payments deficit (we have been importing more than we have been exporting). One of the main reasons for this deficit has been that the government has encouraged the pound to maintain a high value. This reduces the price of imported goods and raises the price of exports. The government could have reversed this process by selling pounds internationally but chose not to do so. The pound has fallen back a little recently but there is little chance of the government allowing this process to go very far . . .'

QUESTIONS

1 Which section of the population would you expect to have beenefited from the 'shift [of] the burden of taxation from direct to indirect taxes'? Explain your answer. (3)
2 Name one advantage and one disadvantage for Dai from this process. (2)
3 How, briefly, have the government's policies for bringing down inflation changed over the years since 1979? (5)
4 How would Dai expect to benefit from the reduction in taxation if he were an exporter? How might he benefit in his building business? (3)
5 Dai will not have liked the general rise in interest rates. Why? Explain your answer fully. (3)
6 'A high value for sterling will bring inflation down but will increase unemployment.' Explain. (3)
7 Discuss the effects of your answer to question 6 on Dai's business. (3)
8 Why do you think that the Conservative government is unlikely to allow the pound to fall too far – given what you know about its *main* aim? (3)
9 Summarise the report under the four headings: Taxes, Inflation, Interest rates and Exchange rates. Divide your page into two – one side headed 'Good developments for business' and the other headed 'Bad developments for business'. Go through the report and your summary and place each thing that has happened – or is expected to happen – into one of the categories. If you think that a development has both good and bad sides place it into both with a note in brackets afterwards explaining what is good *and* bad about it. (10)

(35)

Fig. 7.21 Budget day

8.1 The banking system

A diagram of the banking system in this country would look something like that shown in Fig. 8.1.

The Bank of England

This is the 'bankers' bank' and also the government's bank. It arranges government borrowing and helps carry out its 'monetary policy'.

Discount houses

They act as short-term borrowers from industry, and use the money raised to purchase such assets as government bonds. They also discount **bills of exchange** for firms. A bill of exchange is an IOU to pay for goods that companies can issue and agree to pay at a future date, usually in three months. If the firm wants the money immediately, however, it can take the bill to a discount house who will buy it at a 'discount', i.e. they will pay less than the face value to provide themselves with a profit.

Merchant banks

These are really 'companies' banks'. They advise companies and help them to raise finance. They have a few individual customers, but only those able to deposit more than £25,000!

Clearing banks

Most of us deposit our money with these banks. They have two main types of account:

1 **Current account**
   This is the account that most of us use for our **spending.** We can withdraw money from it at any time but it does not pay interest on the money we may have in our accounts. However, most banks now offer current account deals that *do* pay some interest.

2 **Deposit account**
   This is a **savings** account. The bank can ask for seven days' notice for a withdrawal but it does pay interest.

If we take more money out of our account than we have in it we are said to have an **overdraft.** It is possible to agree with the bank to have an overdraft up to a certain time period and up to a certain limit. In return we pay interest to the bank.

The other way of borrowing money from the bank is in the form of a **loan.** This is a fixed amount that is paid off at regular intervals in regular amounts. The rate of interest on a loan will usually be lower than that on an overdraft because the latter allows more *flexibility* – you can draw out of it whenever you wish, as long as you do not go beyond the agreed limit.

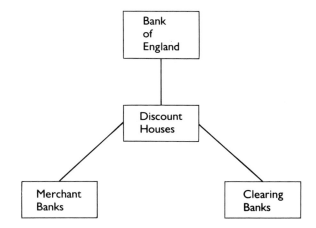

Fig. 8.1   The banking system

Membership of a bank allows you to pay by **cheque** – a piece of paper that 'represents' the money in your account (Fig. 8.2). If there is no money in your account, the bank may not 'honour' the cheque, i.e. they may **bounce** it, which means sending it back to the **drawer** (the person to whom you wrote the cheque). They will write you a stiff letter, and charge you bank charges, as well as leaving you to face the wrath of the shopkeeper! If you have a **cheque card,** however, the bank agrees to honour your cheques up to the value of £50, although they may take the card from you if you misuse it.

The advantage of paying by cheque is that it is convenient and removes the need to carry around large sums of money which may be lost or stolen. It does make fraud more likely, however, and if you lose both your cheque book and cheque card somebody may have a field day with them!

Other means of payment

Increasingly this is becoming the 'age of plastic', especially with the use of **credit cards.** These are even more convenient than cheques and can be used for large or small amounts of money – examples are **Barclaycard Visa,** and **Access.** Again, they must be carefully looked after and they will not 'bounce' unless you go beyond your limit, which may well be more than £1,000. If not used carefully they can be a means of running up debts that cannot be easily paid off. The credit card companies charge high rates of interest on outstanding amounts, i.e. any not paid off within the specified time.

Diner's Club and **American Express** are charge cards. They work just like credit cards but there is no limit on the amount that can be spent. The debt has to be settled in full at the end of each month, however.

Fig. 8.2   The life of a cheque

Building societies

Many people save their money with building societies. The first building society was formed by a group of workmen who pooled their savings to build their own homes. Nowadays they are best known for lending people money to buy houses. They get the money to lend from people who **deposit** money with them. They offer higher rates of interest than the banks, especially if you deposit a large sum of money with them. It used to be less convenient to withdraw money from building societies than from banks, but now they offer similar cheque and cash-card facilities to compete with the banks. The banks are retaliating, though – many of them are now offering people mortgages to buy houses!

ACTIVITY

Imagine that you have £1,000 to invest. Carry out a survey of all the banks and building societies in your high street and see which will offer you the best rate of interest. What is the price in terms of how difficult it is to get at your money? Write a report of your findings.

EXTENSION ACTIVITY

It is possible to earn higher rates of return (or interest) than either banks or building societies can offer by investing in **unit trusts.** These are available from a wide variety of sources and involve your money being invested in shares chosen by a committee – the **trustees.** On the other hand, they are risky – the value of shares can fall as well as rise. Research to find out how you could invest your £1,000 in unit trusts and the advantages and disadvantages of so doing.

8.2 Insurance

Fig. 8.3   The value of insurance

Without insurance, business activity would be impossible. Imagine the following situations:

- You own a warehouse and arrive at work one morning to see that all that remains of your business is piles of ashes and rubble.
- You own a shop; one morning you arrive to find that all your stock has been stolen.
- There is a freak storm one night with hurricane winds. The next morning you find that the roof of your store has been blown off and much of your stock is drenched and unusable.

All of these could happen to any business. Without **insurance cover** the business would be ruined and everything lost. Insurance involves cover for the risk of losing property due to fire, theft and a number of other possible disasters under the heading 'Acts of God' – lightning, earthquakes and hurricanes. There is also, of course, **personal insurance** which covers accidents and deaths of individuals and **vehicle insurance** which covers damage to, and theft of, cars, as well as injury to individuals involved in motor accidents.

Insurance involves everybody with some **risk** pooling their money so that people who do suffer loss will receive **compensation** for it. Everyone pays a **premium** – or contribution to a general fund – organised by an insurance company. If anybody suffers loss they can draw some money out of the fund. One immediate problem with this is the 'fraudulent fire' where somebody deliberately sets fire to a business that might not be doing so well in order to collect the insurance money which is worth more than the business to them. This is a criminal act, however, and is usually punished by imprisonment where detected.

There are four legal principles that govern everything to do with insurance:

1 Insurable interest
The person doing the insuring – the **insuree** – must stand to lose something. In other words, although I can insure my own car, I could not take out insurance for my friend's car.

2 Utmost good faith
This relates to the 'fraudulent fire' example. The insurance claim must be truthful and disclose all the relevant facts. The insurance company, on the other hand, must honour its promises.

3 Indemnity
Nobody should profit by claiming insurance. You are only compensated for the value of what you have lost.

4 Proximate cause
The insurer has to pay for things that are directly related to the accident. This could cover things like damage to windows in the event of a burglary.

Some risks in business are *not* insurable:

- Commercial failure in business, perhaps through failure to attract sufficient customers, cannot be covered.
- Machinery and equipment cannot be insured against 'fair wear and tear' or where the probability of loss is inevitable.

The insurance market

Insurance is carried out by **insurance companies.** They have **agents** who work for them and try to find them business. **Brokers,** on the other hand, do *not* work for insurance companies but act as 'independent advisers', advising clients on the best policy to buy.

Lloyd's of London is a society of underwriters. These are private people who accept insurance business for their own profit (or loss). Frequently these individuals join together as syndicates (groups) to enable them to cover larger risks – such as a jumbo jet.

Underwriters do not deal directly with the general public, but with brokers who act as go-betweens. The usual legal principles associated with insurance apply to insurance at Lloyd's too.

EXERCISE

Hold a class 'brainstorming session' on all the risks that face us in life. Divide up into groups, taking one of these risks each. With the help of your teacher, choose an insurance company and write a polite letter to them asking what protection they can offer you against this risk. You could present a report to the rest of the class when you have the information.

Fig. 8.4 Lloyds of London new building

8.3 Consumer protection

Firms supply us with a very large range of goods and services and in return expect payment. They will generally hope to make as large a profit as possible, and there could be a temptation to 'cut corners' with goods – to produce shoddy goods of a sub-standard quality or to describe them in a misleading way. Therefore it is necessary to have various laws to protect the buyers of goods and services – the **consumer** – from being cheated or misled in any way. In addition, there is a 'voluntary' body called the **Consumers' Association** which looks after the interests of consumers and which publishes a magazine called *Which?*; this journal acts as a 'watchdog' for the consumer and regularly looks at and tests the different brands on offer in a particular market and advises on the best buys. There are several radio and television programmes which serve the same function.

Legislation

A number of laws exist to protect the consumer. You do not need to know them all, but among the more important and up-to-date are the following:

- **Sale of Goods Act (1979)**
  This states that goods must *work* properly and be of 'merchantable quality', conform to the *description* made of them and be fit for their *purpose*.
- **Consumer Safety Act (1978)**
  This controls the sale of goods that may be dangerous.
- **Consumer Credit Act (1974)**
  This controls bodies that offer credit terms to the consumer. The Act compels them to ensure that the borrower knows all the information that is relevant – no rising rate of interest 'in small print' – and forces them to charge a 'reasonable' rate of interest. *All* credit agreements must be registered with the Office of Fair Trading.

EXERCISE

1 Which section of the Sale of Goods Act (1979) would each of the following goods be liable under (work, description or purpose)?
  (a) a weak sauce that states on the front label '*strong and spicy*';
  (b) a train set that keeps breaking down;
  (c) a stove that cannot be used for baking;
  (d) a doll that comes apart at the seams immediately after being bought;
  (e) a vacuum cleaner that breaks down after being regularly used for five years.
2 Think of *five* goods that might be covered by the Consumer Safety Act (1978).

The following story appeared in *Which?* (November 1987).

Piano faulty

The Smiths needed a piano that was in good enough condition to take their children up to Grade 8 in their piano exams. They stressed this to the saleswoman in the shop when they bought a second-hand Welmar piano for £1,119. The saleswoman had told them it was. She also sent them a picture of a Welmar piano and had written beneath it FIRST CLASS CONDITION – £1,119. About a month later a professional tuner discovered a long list of faults. Although the outer casing was in good condition many parts inside were very badly worn. He said that it would cost several hundred pounds to have the piano repaired . . . .

The sellers wrote back to Mr Smith saying that the piano was reasonably priced considering its age and condition. They offered to carry out the repairs but said that they would have to charge. When Mr Smith consulted *Which?* they told him that the sellers were in breach of the Sale of Goods Act (1979) because the piano was not in first-class condition as the saleswoman had described it – *description* – and also that the faults found by the tuner seemed to indicate that the piano was not fit for its *purpose*. They prepared a letter for Mr Smith to send to the sellers, asking them either to carry out the repairs free or refund his money . . . .

The sellers did not reply to this letter, so *Which?* advised Mr Smith to get an estimate from another firm for repair which totalled £390. *Which?* drafted a letter for him to send to the sellers saying that he would have the repairs done by the other firm and claim £390 from them in the **County Court.** The sellers replied offering either a contribution of £100 to the cost of repairs or to give him a full refund and take the piano back. Mr Smith chose the refund and has bought another piano.

EXERCISE

1 The first thing that Mr Smith did was to write to the shop complaining about the way in which he had been misled. Draft a letter of complaint that he might have sent. (Obviously you don't know the details of the faults of the piano; write a short general letter of complaint from the facts that are available in the first paragraph of the extract.)

2 Draft the letter that *Which?* might have prepared for Mr Smith (see the second paragraph) explaining to the sellers how they have breached the Sale of Goods Act (1979). Use a typewriter or word processor if one is available.

3 With the help of the extract, write a short essay explaining exactly what the Sale of Goods Act (1979) is and why it is very important for protecting consumers. What would have happened to Mr Smith if it had not existed?

8.4 Health and Safety at work

Another area in business over which the government has some control is that of health and safety at work. Over the years several Acts have been passed which try to ensure that the conditions in which people work are safe and do not endanger their health. Obviously this is easier to bring about in some industries than in others.

The main legislation that covers this is the **Health and Safety at Work Act (1974).** This Act covers 'basic obligations' of both employers and employees and 'general obligations' of everybody.

The employer is expected to uphold ' . . . the duty . . . to ensure health, safety and welfare at work for all his employees'.

To achieve this, employers are expected to provide (among other things):

- healthy and safe systems at work;
- healthy and safe working environment;
- safe plant, machinery, equipment and appliances and maintain them in good order;
- safe methods for handling, storing and transporting materials;
- adequate instruction and training for employees;
- adequate supervision by competent personnel.

Employees are expected to follow these guidelines:

- to act in the course of their employment with due care for the health and safety of themselves, other workers and the general public;
- to observe the provisions of the Act wherever applicable to them or matters within their control;
- to co-operate with the employer so far as it is necessary to enable that duty to be carried out.

The 'general obligations' on everybody are:

- No person shall interfere with or misuse anything provided in the interests of health, safety and welfare.
- No employer shall levy on any employee any charge in respect of anything provided to meet the legal requirements.

EXERCISE

1 Try to think of *three* types of work that are likely to be dangerous whatever rules there are and *three* types of work that really should be safe. Explain your answer in each case.

2 Read carefully through the provisions of the Health and Safety at Work Act (1974) given above and, to ensure that you understand them, write out a short explanation of what each means in your own words. You might want to discuss them with your teacher first.

Most places of work will have a **safety representative** whose job as the workers' representative is to ensure that the Act is being followed and to 'investigate potential hazards and dangerous occurrences at the workplace . . . and to examine the causes of accidents at the workplace'. Basically the representative negotiates on safety matters with the employer and tries to get the best deal possible for the workers – as trade unions do over pay and conditions (see Unit 4, Section 4.6).

EXERCISE

Read through the following piece and try to pick out as many examples as possible in which the Health and Safety at Work Act (1974) is being broken. Suggest a remedy for each example you find. Put your conclusions in the form of a report to the management of the firm.

I had been asked to come to visit the offices of Brown, Brown, Brown and Brown Solicitors because of my experience as a safety representative in another office. I don't know what areas of law they specialised in – but it most certainly was not health and safety.

The offices were on the first floor. The stair carpet was terribly worn and I almost fell over on the second stair from the top because a tack was loose.

It was difficult to walk along the corridor at the top leading to the office door; there were several pieces of furniture which I think were waiting to be thrown out. I was told by my guide that they had been 'waiting' for about four weeks already. A bulb had gone in the corridor which did not make crossing it any easier.

I was almost knocked down as I was about to enter the reception area. It was a 'swing door' but the glass was not very clear so the person who happened to be coming out at the same time as I was entering could not see me and swung the door somewhat wildly at me. He was terribly apologetic.

I was taken through the reception area into the front office. There was a filing cabinet just behind the door. Unfortunately someone had left a middle drawer open. I walked straight into it causing a sharp, burning sensation in my stomach which lasted for some hours. Had the sharp corner of the drawer caught me it could have been much nastier. By this stage I was beginning to wonder if it wasn't time to go while I was still alive.

I was offered a cup of coffee – possibly to calm my nerves. As I was sitting at a desk drinking it I noticed two burning cigarettes that had been left in an ashtray. They were sharing it with a number of screwed-up pieces of paper. When I had finished my coffee I wandered into the next office. The photocopier and other equipment was kept in here. There was a young

Fig. 8.5 Breaking the Health and Safety at Work Act

lad trying to do some photocopying. He didn't really seem to know what he was doing until I showed him. What was particularly worrying was that he didn't realise how important it was to put the cover down and keep your eyes well away from the light before switching on. He seemed a little concerned when I told him that someone in the office where I worked had been semi-blinded by a photo-copier.

I thought that I would ask a few questions of the staff about fire arrangements – what the 'procedure' was in case of fire, where the fire doors were, where the fire extinguishers were. They looked at me blankly and said, 'You had better ask the boss. We don't know.' I decided that I most definitely would.

EXTENSION ACTIVITY

Most places of work will have a Health and Safety Officer. Research to find a firm in your area that employs one. Write a polite letter asking if you could interview him or her about the job. Useful questions to ask include the following:
■ What are the particular hazards that his or her workers face and how does he or she try to reduce them?
■ Are the employers co-operative or not?
■ How does the Health and Safety at Work Act (1974) apply to them?

One place where you are sure to find a Health and Safety Officer, of course, is in your own school. Try to find out which member of staff is responsible for this job and one of you, at least, could interview him or her.

Alternatively, you could draw up a questionnaire as a result of a class discussion and send it to a firm – with a letter explaining what you are doing – to find out how they deal with health and safety at work.

8.5 Pressure groups on business

In addition to the effects of government legislation there are other, 'unofficial', groups who attempt to exert influence over business decisions. Many of them are concerned with the **environmental** effects of industry – in other words, the effect on the surrounding area, wildlife, the atmosphere, and the general pollution that industry can cause. One of the best known of these is **Friends of the Earth,** which is a group of people who are dedicated to protecting our environment from the effects of pollution – minimising the **social costs** (see Unit 1, Section 1.5).

The best way to see the causes that such groups fight is to look at a particular example.

Nuclear power at Druridge Bay

The Central Electricity Generating Board wants to build a nuclear power station at Druridge Bay which is a stretch of coastline in Northumberland. Of course the CEGB is owned by the government and so is really a 'nationalised industry' (although the current government has plans to 'privatise' electricity with possibly interesting results for the nuclear-power station building programme). Thus it does not conform to the usual 'commercial' rules of business such as profit maximisation. Nevertheless, the arguments over the siting of nuclear power stations, in terms of environmental effects, pollution, safety and social benefits and costs mirror those in other industries.

The CEGB argues that the demand for electricity in England is rising and that our means for satisfying that demand is not. Coal is one fuel that can be burned to make electricity but we have **finite** (limited) supplies of it. The other 'fuel' that can be used is uranium which, when its atoms are split, creates an awful lot of energy. Supplies of uranium are enormous. The CEGB claims that nuclear power, as this is called, is cheap and safe. How many miners are killed and injured while digging for coal? Coal-fired power stations pollute the atmosphere, damaging people's lungs and perhaps causing acid rain. If we abandoned our nuclear programme the cost of electricity would rise and we would have great problems in meeting our energy needs in the future.

There are a whole number of 'pressure groups' who are campaigning against the plan. In addition to Friends of the Earth there are groups like **Greenpeace,** who are opposed to all nuclear power, as well as local pressure groups such as the **Tyneside Anti-Nuclear Campaign** and the very local **Druridge Bay Action Committee** which was formed especially to oppose the siting of the power station at Druridge Bay. They claim that our energy needs can be met in other ways; apart from coal – of which they say there is still plenty – there are 'alternative energy sources' such as **solar power** (power from the rays of the sun), **wave power** and **wind power** – all of which are **infinite,** i.e. they will last for ever. They claim that the building of a power station at Druridge Bay will ruin a beautiful area, one that has been designated 'of outstanding natural beauty' (see Fig. 8.6). Their main argument, however, is that nuclear power just is not safe and poses unacceptable risks both to the immediate inhabitants of the area and to the atmosphere as a whole.

Fig. 8.6   Druridge Bay

The splitting of the atoms in uranium produces radioactive rays that cause cancer and death if they escape into the atmosphere, and accidents such as those that occurred at Three Mile Island in America and Chernobyl in the USSR are proof of this; the rays from the latter killed people in the Soviet Union and spread across Europe, causing danger in a number of countries. Even without accidents they claim that figures show higher rates of leukaemia in children who live in areas near nuclear power stations.

As you can see, there are strong arguments on either side, and one short chapter can only scratch the surface. The point is, however, that businesses do not take decisions about where to locate 'in a vacuum', but are subject to many pressures from different groups. The anti-nuclear campaigners organise petitions, demonstrations and lobbying of Members of Parliament. In the last resort what happens really depends on the government; possibly a Conservative government would be more sympathetic to the case for nuclear power than would be a Labour or Democrat government. Governments are elected by the people, however, so well-organised pressure can persuade them to follow a certain course.

EXERCISE

Try to work out all the possible **social benefits** and all the **social costs** of the siting of a nuclear power station at Druridge Bay for:
(a) the local inhabitants;
(b) the country as a whole.

EXTENSION ACTIVITY

Research to find out more about the nuclear power programme in this country and, particularly, the proposed site at Druridge Bay. Write to the organisations mentioned in this chapter for a start and they will give you more addresses. This could be a topic for a GCSE project.

Fig. 8.7   The Chernobyl disaster

Footnote:
Students at Seaton Burn High School just outside Newcastle-upon-Tyne investigated this topic as a GCSE project. As part of their research they surveyed the views of local people in nearby Ashington. They interviewed a total of 85 people and tried to make their sample as representative as possible. They found that most people did not want a nuclear power station at Druridge Bay (92 per cent of those interviewed) and that half of them planned to leave the area if the station were built. About 45 per cent of the sample thought that existing stations should be kept but no more built and 31 per cent of people thought that existing nuclear stations should be dismantled.

9.1 The microprocessor and information technology

As we are often told, this is the age of the computer. Computers have been in use in industry for the last 40 years but until the 1970s they were very large, expensive machines which needed a whole airconditioned room to themselves. Then came the silicon chip and miniaturisation. The machines became smaller and cheaper, to the extent that many executives now have their own desk-top personal computer (PC).

Fig. 9.1

What is a microprocessor?

At the heart of every microprocessor is a tiny silicon chip. On it are printed the circuits which store the many millions of characters of memory. A microprocessor can do arithmetic, re-arrange letters and select and organise information.

There are three basic stages through which information passes: **input – process – output**

1 Input

This refers to the entering of information into a computer. The device most commonly used is a keyboard, similar to that found on a typewriter (Fig. 9.1).

2 Process

The central processing unit (CPU) does this. It stores information and carries out the instructions of the operator. The CPU houses the memory and the logic unit which carries out any mathematical operations. The information is actually stored on disks. These are metal plates, with magnetic properties, that are divided into tracks – rather like a record.

3 Output

The output is 'getting back' or retrieving information. This can be seen on the television-like screen that most microprocessors have – the visual display unit (VDU). To get 'hard copy' a printer is needed.

Microprocessors now have very many uses in business. We shall look briefly at three of them.

Word processing

This is the use of computers for the purpose of producing correspondence documents. **Word processors** are increasingly replacing typewriters and have a number of advantages:

Fig. 9.2   Central processing unit

- They are easy to operate.
- Corrections can easily be made and the layout altered before the document is printed.
- Copies and records of work done can be stored on disk without taking up valuable office space – no need for packed filing cabinets. This should make information much easier to find.

Fig. 9.3   Computer vdu

EXERCISE

If you have access to a word processor copy out the section 'What is a microprocessor?' as far as the end of point 3. Print it out, then recall your work to the screen and make the following changes:
(a) Delete the word 'many' in line 2.
(b) Replace the words 'similar to' in line 10 with 'like'.
(c) Insert the word 'complicated' before 'mathematical' in line 16.

(d) Delete the whole of point 1 – **Input** – and swop round (transpose) the next two points, remembering to renumber them.
(e) Obtain a print-out of your amended work.

Data bases

A **data base** is a bank of information that is organised under certain headings – **fields** – to make it more easily accessible. A **search** can be carried out on the data base so that the user can extract certain pieces of information easily and quickly.

EXERCISE

We have already met Winston Brown, the owner of a car sales business, in Unit 5. He wants to keep a record of all the people who have sold him cars so that he can build up a list of potential suppliers and the sort of cars that he might get from them. He needs their *names,* the *towns* in which they live, the *make* of car that they sold him, its *cc* and *registration number.*
This information is given in the table below. Create a data file with this information on it.
   Carry out the following searches and obtain a hard copy of each piece of information:
(a) all the people who sold Ford Fiestas;
(b) all the customers from Blaydon;
(c) all the customers from Blaydon who sold Ford Fiestas;
(d) all the cars with a cc of 1500 – just print the make of the car and the cc;
(e) all the customers from Newcastle with Ford Fiestas of less than 1000 cc. Just print their names, the town, the make and the cc.

Spreadsheets

A **spreadsheet** is like a sheet of squared paper, divided into rows and columns into which numbers or words can be inserted. If used correctly spreadsheets will carry out many tedious and complex calculations.

Name	Town	Make	CC	Reg. No.
K. Stevens	Blaydon	Ford Fiesta	950	B426 ABC
M. Philpott	Newcastle	Ford Sierra	1500	B146 GHB
F. Greystock	Newcastle	Fiat Uno	1000	SRJ 855X
B. Wilkinson	Alnwick	Renault 25	1500	A426 DHY
O. Wright	Blaydon	Ford Fiesta	1500	ACD 221W
M. Gardiner	Blythe	Porsche	2000	A567 LOM
W. Henley	Bedlington	Ford Fiesta	1200	B456 YHU
W. Banks	Widrington	Ford Escort	1500	C567 IUH
Q. Smith	Morpeth	Peugeot	1200	C297 JIM
S. Hunt	Newcastle	Ford Fiesta	950	A290 SCF
G. Hall	Blaydon	Ford Sierra	1000	B389 ITF
J. Alton	Blaydon	Ford Fiesta	950	C567 PLK
D. Thorpe	Hexham	Ford Sierra	1500	B214 TYU
S. Tooley	Newcastle	Ford Escort	950	C695 IHL
F. Rogers	Blaydon	Fiat Uno	1000	A908 KLO

EXERCISE

Let us again go back to Winston Brown's car-sales business and, in particular, his **cash flow budget** (Unit 5, Section 5.3). You can insert the figures for sales, and all the different costs, and then let the computer calculate **total inflow, total outflow** and the **closing balance** by putting in the correct **formula** in January and then copying it for the rest of the months. So:

$$Total\ Inflow = Opening\ Balance + Sales$$
$$Total\ Outflow = Rent + Wages + Heat\ and\ Light$$
$$+ General + Supplies + Vehicle$$
$$Closing\ Balance = Total\ Inflow - Total\ Outflow$$

One of the uses of a spreadsheet in business is to answer 'What would happen if . . . ?' questions. You can see the power of a spreadsheet if you carry out the following changes:

What if . . .
- Sales for each month were £100 higher?
- Rent in March was £10 higher?
- The vehicle had not been bought?
- There has been a miscalculation – suppliers are only £450 per month?
- A new machine was bought in June for £750?

Make a note of the new profit closing balance for June after each of these changes. The spreadsheet has, of course, calculated it for you. You should be able to see how useful this is for a business with complex accounts and budgets!

Other uses for computers

Computers today are so powerful and sophisticated that they have many uses outside the business office. Recent developments have been in the area of design – **computer aided design (CAD)**. All forms of design work previously carried out on the drawing board can now be done on computers. A **mouse** is a device that moves the cursor around the screen 'from the desk'. It is particularly useful as part of CAD when it is necessary to draw on the screen. A **light pen**, on the other hand, draws directly onto the screen. **Touch screens** have been developed which give information 'at a touch'. The effects on business of these developments will be far-reaching.

9.2 Information technology: Wider uses and applications

Apart from its use in business, information technology, in various forms, is now widely used elsewhere. The **police, educational establishments, social services, immigration** and **social security** all benefit from the use of microprocessors to keep records – in a similar way to that shown for data bases in the previous section. This is obviously a far more efficient way of keeping records than on paper; it takes up far less space, the information is not likely to be lost (unless there is a power failure – but most systems will have **back-up** facilities to protect the data) and it can be easily retrieved and manipulated.

There is good reason to be concerned about this, however. People will be concerned to know exactly *where* information is being held about them and *what* that information is. In other words, the growth of personal information stored on computers is seen as being a possible **threat to privacy.** As a result of fears of this kind, the government passed the **Data Protection Act** in 1984; its main provision – the right to know what information is stored about you on computers – finally came into effect in November 1987.

Fig. 9.4   A large, computerised institution

There are six main data protection principles. Organisations using computers are required to ensure that all personal information is:

1   collected and processed fairly and lawfully;
2   held only for purposes that are lawful and are described in the Data Register entry made by the organisation (The Data Register is a body that all organisations holding personal records on computer must register with. However, the registrar estimates that there could be up to 100,000 organisations that have not registered. It is now a criminal offence to fail to do so.);
3   adequate, relevant and not excessive in relation to the purposes for which it is being held;
4   accurate and, where necessary, kept up to date;
5   protected by proper security.

The Act gives individuals five rights:

1   to check if any organisation keeps information about them on computer;
2   to see a copy of the information, subject to certain exemptions;
3   to complain to the Data Registrar or the courts if a person does not like the way organisations are collecting or using the personal information on computer;
4   to have inaccurate computer records corrected or deleted;
5   to seek compensation for damage resulting from the misuse of computer records.

The diagram in Fig. 9.5 shows simply how to complain if you think that information is wrongfully being held on computer.

Let us look briefly at some of the areas in which computers are used and the difference that the Data Protection Act makes.

Police

Use: There is a **police national computer** that keeps information under seven categories; there is also a local police computer that stores information on it – obviously of a more local nature.
Difference: Anyone now has the right to ask his or her local force whether any personal information is being stored, either on the local computer or on the police national computer. Each search under just one category will cost £10.

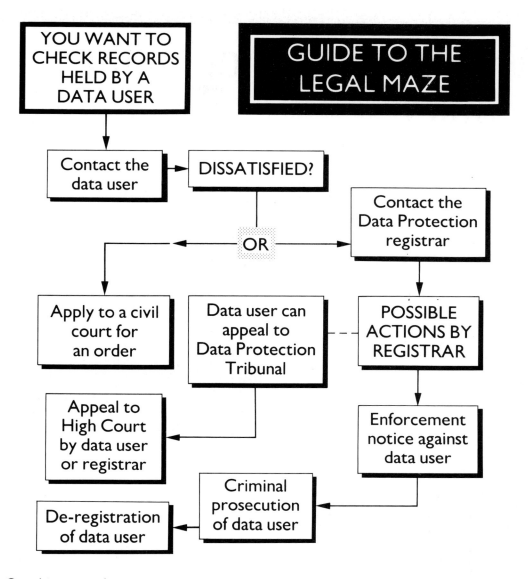

Fig. 9.5   Complaints procedure

Educational establishments

Use: Most schools have records of such things as children's backgrounds, previous schools, medical history, learning progress, etc.
Difference: School, and university, students and parents now have access to these records *if they are kept on computer;* the problem is that most school records are still kept on paper and there is no right of access to these.

Social services

Use: Many general practitioners and most hospitals now keep patients' records on computers.
Difference: Individual health records can still be withheld if it can be proved that disclosure would cause 'serious harm' to anybody.

Immigration

Use: The records of immigrants, including suspected illegal immigrants, are held on the Home Office computer.
Difference: A written application must be made to the Home Office to see any of these files. The only exemptions are the possibility that disclosure may hinder the 'prevention or detection of crime'.

Social Security

At the time of writing, little information on Social Security is held on computer. The Department of Health is planning a £1.6 billion computerisation programme over the five-year period 1987–92.

Any information can be withheld on the grounds of **national security,** however; in other words if the disclosure is believed to reduce the security of the country it can be withheld.

9.3 Communication in the office

In any business, communication between people is essential. **Internally,** most firms will use the following forms of communication:

- the spoken word;
- the memorandum;
- the telephone.

Externally, formal communication methods include the following:

- the letter;
- the telephone;
- telex and fax machines.

The spoken word

This is the original, most straightforward means of exchanging information. It has many advantages: you are talking to the person *directly* and so there is less chance of misunderstanding and confusion about what is being said: *eye contact* can make a message stronger and *body signals* can help to put across the 'unspoken message'. For example:

> John was called into the manager's office. He had been doing nothing 'wrong' but he was working slowly, was making a number of mistakes in his work and was generally giving the impression that his 'heart wasn't in it'. The manager talked to him about his work and tried to find out what the problem was. John did not really know and said so. The manager was sympathetic and tried to help and understand. His *tone* and the way in which he looked at John implied that his patience was wearing out, however, and John knew, when he left the office, that if there was not an improvement soon he would find himself out of a job.

The spoken word is also the obvious method of communication when several individuals within a company (or group of companies) meet together – board meetings, management meetings, departmental meetings, etc. all depend on people communicating verbally.

Of course, the spoken word has its limitations. At present, a face-to-face conversation can only take place with somebody in the same room. (Video-phones will be in use in the near future, but that is another story!) As a means of problem-solving and decision-making *within* a company it is probably still the best means of communication – people always respond better to a 'face-to-face' meeting.

Fig. 9.6

EXERCISE

Divide into pairs and make up a dialogue that might apply in the talk between John and the manager. Rehearse it together and then act it out in front of the class. Remember the important thing is not so much *what* is said but *how* it is said and the 'body language' that is used to put the real message across.

The memorandum

Note the layout. The **memorandum,** or 'memo', will usually show at the top *to whom* it is being sent, who it is *from,* a *reference*, a *date* and a *subject*. As you can see, there is no 'Dear Sir/Madam' or 'Yours faithfully/sincerely' or any kind of greeting on a memorandum – it should be brief and to the point.

A memorandum is usually sent as a confirmation of a decision to somebody within the company. It is also used as a reminder; an internal request; a source of information to be circulated to other, interested personnel within a company so that everybody concerned knows what's going on in other departments.

It is a formal way of making contact and so can appear a little unfriendly – especially when the people concerned know each other well and work together. However, as a way of confirming verbal decisions or when people are busy and find it difficult to see each other it is both useful and helpful.

```
MEMORANDUM                                    Ref: PD/AS

To:      Don Willis                           Date:  8 July

From:    Philippa Darwin

Subject: Oasis Pool site

As you couldn't get back from Glasgow in time, I arranged meeting
with sub-contractors to discuss delay in completion of the
swimming-pool project.  Their Managing Director and Site Manager
will be with us at 10.15 am tomorrow (Friday) when we will go
through all details, costs, complaints, etc.  Please make sure
all personnel concerned with this project are in the boardroom by
9.45 am so that we can have a preliminary discussion - we can't
afford to lose such an important customer as the Bellevue
Building Group.
```

Fig. 9.7   A memorandum

EXERCISE

Prepare a memorandum from yourself to a classmate reminding them that they have borrowed your exercise book and requesting its prompt return for a reason that you can make up. Use your initials as a reference and put in today's date.

How would you feel if *you* received a memo like this – especially from somebody whom you saw every day?

The letter

If you are writing to somebody outside the firm, you would communicate by **letter**. Read through the letter in Fig. 9.8.

Note the following about the layout of the letter:

- The addresses and the date are in **open punctuation;** this is the style usually adopted today – no commas or full stops and just the number in the date (no 'th'). The greeting at the top of the letter is also in open punctuation.
- There is a line space between each paragraph and the first word of each paragraph is set full out to the left.
- As the letter was addressed to a specified individual – Mrs Finnegan – the sender closes with 'Yours sincerely'. If the letter is addressed only to a department of a firm, or the firm itself – i.e. if the receiver's name is not known – the letter would start 'Dear Sirs' in the case of a firm, or 'Dear Sir/Madam' to an unknown individual, for example the Sales Manager, and would finish 'Yours faithfully'.
- Sufficient space is left between the closing greeting and the sender's name and job title for the sender to sign the letter.

EXERCISE

1 Why do you think Mrs Finnegan sent a letter originally on 12 November?
2 What method of transport would you expect to have been used to bring the plastics from Ireland ? Explain your answer.
3 It is possible that Brown & Sons Ltd have a cash flow problem. Will delaying payment for two months help? If so, why?
4 Why would you expect Mrs Finnegan to allow this despite her apparent preference for quicker payment?
5 Draft the letter that Mrs Finnegan may have sent on 12 November. Use the same format you have been shown here and try to adopt the same business-like tone. If you have access to a typewriter or a word processor use it for your letter.

BROWN & SONS TOYMAKERS LTD
Gubbat Street
Littletown
Eastshire E18 7JB
Tel: 0909–456832

23 November 1988

Mrs J Finnegan
Irish Plastics Ltd
Dowden Street
Dublin 12
EIRE

Our ref: FS/CJ

Dear Mrs Finnegan

Thank you for your letter of 12 November. I am now able to confirm that the consignment of plastics has arrived and can only think that it was held up by transport difficulties. I shall be making enquiries with our carriers.

As agreed with you, we will settle your invoice within two months. This is the usual credit period allowed to us by our other suppliers.

May I thank you for the trouble you have taken. I look forward to further dealings between your companies.

Yours sincerely

Freda Smith (Ms)
Purchasing Manager

Fig. 9.8

The telephone

It is possible, of course, to speak to someone almost anywhere in the world on the **telephone**. It is a **two-way** form of communication – you speak to someone and they speak back to you straightaway. Its drawbacks are that you cannot leave a message on a telephone if the person to whom you wish to speak is not there – although you can leave a message with anyone else who happens to be there; the effectiveness of that depends upon his or her accuracy in taking down what you say and being sure that the message is passed on to the person concerned. The development of **answering machines** where you *can* leave a message partly gets over that problem. The major problem with the telephone is that you are *not* talking 'face to face' and so miss out on the advantages that have been mentioned for that.

The old idea of a telephone being used in a particular room is being replaced with **mobile** telephones. These can only be used within a limited distance of the home base, however. **Cellular** telephones, on the other hand, operate on radio waves and can be used anywhere.

Fig. 9.9

Telex and fax

Telex machines provide a quick means of communication – combining the speed of the telephone with the accuracy of the printed word. The message is typed into the machine, changed into electronic signals, and passed down a telephone line to the teleprinter at the other end. Calls may be made to any telex subscriber worldwide and it does not matter if no one is in the office so long as the teleprinter is switched on. The message is available when the operator returns.

Fax (facsimile transmission) is very similar except it combines the copying ability of a photocopier with the speed of a telephone link.

Computer networks

Increasingly computers are being used to *send* information as well as to *store* it. If computers in different places are linked by cable (networked) then messages can be sent between them. The most common form of this is **electronic mail** which can link factories, offices and other places of work. The message is typed into the computer, posted to a central computer, and stored until the user asks to see the mail when it is displayed on the receiver's terminal. Electronic mail has the advantage that the message is sent instantaneously (no postal delay) and can be picked up when the recipient wishes.

Other communication services offered through computer networks are **Oracle, Ceefax** and **Prestel:**

- **Oracle and Ceefax**
  These are 'magazines' that can be read on your own television screen; Oracle is shown on the ITV channels and Ceefax on BBC channels. They are very much a **one-way** means of communication, however; the user cannot give any information back. These are known as **teletext** services.

- **Prestel**
  It is possible both to give information to, and receive information from, Prestel. Holiday bookings, ordering goods, etc. can all be done through the Prestel service. Communication is two-way or **inter-active**. Prestel is a **videotext** service.

EXERCISE

Go through each of the methods of communications that have been mentioned in this section. Describe them briefly in your own words and pick out the advantages and disadvantages of each. For each one think of *two* business situations in which they might be of use. Explain your reasons for your choice.

Fig. 9.10

Fig. 9.11

10.1 Westfield and Sons Ltd

The firm of Westfield and Sons Ltd makes spare parts for tractors. It has been in existence for fifty years and was founded by the present Managing Director's father. It has always been primarily a family business but has expanded to the extent that it employs a workforce of 120. While not earning enormous profits it more than breaks even, having a comfortable margin of safety in its production and earning sufficient dividends per share to keep its shareholders – mainly members of the family – happy.

John Westfield, the founder's son, is the Chairman and chief shareholder. His brother James, a younger son, is the General Manager and is directly responsible for the day-to-day running of the company; he also owns a substantial number of shares. The other main managers are not members of the family: Harry Smith is the Chief Accountant; Gill Fairfax is the Personnel Officer; John Roberts is in charge of Purchasing; Kay Salmon is the Chief Engineer; Phil Logan is Production Manager; Keith Storey is in charge of Marketing and Faith Hope runs the Research and Development Department.

1 Make a brief note explaining the part that each person will play in the running of the business. (9)

2 Harry Smith has two assistants (accounting technicians), Gill Fairfax has one, Kay Salmon has three, Keith Storey has two and Faith Hope has two. Draw up a clearly labelled organisation tree for Westfield and Sons Ltd, using as much of the given information as you think is relevant. (10)

3 Explain why you think that they have not concentrated on earning 'enormous profits', showing that you fully understand the accounting terms that were used in the opening paragraph. (6)

As an example of their financial policy we can look at the figures that Harry used to draw up the Profit and Loss Account for 1987. He knew that their wage bill was £66,565, their power bills totalled £22,432, their sales brought in £287,980, their transport bills were £15,007 and that they were paying an annual rate of interest of 11 per cent on a loan of £25,000. The cost of the sales was £75,693 and all other expenses totalled £11,200.

4 These figures have obviously arrived on Harry's desk in a bit of a mess. Sort them out so that you can calculate:
(a) the gross profit; (2)
(b) the net profit; (2)

5 If the capital at the start of the financial year was £150,000, calculate the rate of return on capital. What does this tell us about the state of the business? (5)

The figures for the Balance Sheet are also rather muddled. Harry knows that on 31 December 1987 the company owes £5,000 to the bank in addition to the loan already mentioned. Its land and buildings are worth £90,000, it is owed £23,000 in unpaid bills and has stock and semi-finished goods worth £31,590. The capital currently invested is £150,000 and you have already calculated the retained profit. Fixtures and fittings and equipment are worth £47,876 and the company has investments of £23,602. The company has holdings of cash of £58,265.

6 Using this information, draw up a Balance Sheet for the firm as of 31 December 1987, setting it out in a vertical format. From this Balance Sheet calculate:
(a) the net working capital; (3)
(b) the capital owned; (3)
(c) the current ratio; (3)
(d) the acid test ratio. (3)
Write a short note explaining what each tells us about the business, being particularly careful to distinguish between (a) and (b) on the one hand and (c) and (d) on the other. (5)

The general 'economic situation' was becoming of increasing concern to the Westfields. The government was determined to 'reduce inflation' and to help it achieve that was reducing the money supply to a great extent and cutting government expenditure. It was also raising interest rates which kept the value of the pound high. This was particularly damaging to Westfield and Sons Ltd, who sold quite a lot of output abroad – mainly in developing countries.

7 Inflation is not good for business. Give *three* reasons why Westfield and Sons Ltd might welcome its reduction. (3)

8 Explain why the government has been 'reducing the money supply . . . and cutting government expenditure' to bring inflation down. Are there any other policies that the government could follow? (5)

9 Why did the government raise interest rates and how does this affect business? (3)

10 Why did the government also want to keep the value of the pound high as part of its anti-inflationary policy? Why would this particularly affect a firm like Westfield and Sons which sells a lot of its output abroad? Try to explain why the effect of this on Westfield's business would be particularly bad if there were a number of other countries also trying to sell tractor parts to developing countries. (8)

11 Compose a letter that John Westfield might send to the Prime Minister welcoming the attempt to reduce inflation but pointing out the bad effects of the policies used on his business and suggesting an alternative method of achieving the same result.
(10)

(80)

10.2 John Jones

Fig. 10.1

John Jones had always wanted to work for himself; the opportunity arose when a relative died and left him a sum of money. He used it to buy a disused garage and some tools for his picture-framing business. This had been a hobby of his for some time and he had done quite a lot of work for friends so his name was quite widely known in the area. He was very excited about the prospect of working for himself, although he had a number of worries – principally about the consequences for himself if the business was not a success.

1 Explain clearly how the work that he had already done for friends would help him when starting his business. (5)
2 What would you expect to excite him about the prospect of working for himself? (6)
3 What might you expect to worry him? (6)
4 Suggest *three* other sources of finance that are available to people when they start a business – at least one must be a government or local authority body. (6)
5 There would be both advantages and disadvantages for him in taking a partner to run the business with him. Write a letter to John *either* trying to persuade him to take on a partner *or* trying to dissuade him from it. (8)

John found that his sales grew steadily, although the amount of credit he was forced to allow his customers on occasion caused him 'cash flow problems'. He felt that, before expanding further, he needed to embark on some market research, as he was not entirely sure which frames were the most popular. He also felt that the frame service that he was offering needed to be more widely known so he decided to embark on a local advertising campaign.

6 Show exactly how market research would enable him to expand. How would you expect him to carry out that market research? (10)

7 Why did he need to advertise? What advertising media would be most appropriate in this situation? What other factors would he need to take into account when deciding on his campaign? (10)

We have mentioned John's 'cash flow problems'. To help him resolve them an accountant friend of his helped him to draw up a **cash flow budget** for the first year of trading.

8 Explain exactly what a cash flow budget is and how it would help him solve the problem. (3)

John gave the following figures to his accountant friend:

His rates are £55 per month, his power bills £120 per quarter; he buys in £190 worth of wood per month – this rose to £210 in the last three months of the year. His suppliers allow him one month's credit. On average he spends £40 per month buying and repairing equipment. When he started in business he took out a small bank loan; he is paying this back at a rate of £30 per quarter.

His sales figures are as follows:

Jan. £250, Feb. £250, Mar. £300, Apr. £320, May £400, June £600, July £700, Aug. £700, Sept. £750, Oct. £400, Nov. £600, Dec. £650.

He allows his customers one month's credit.

9 Using the information given above, draw up a cash flow budget for John's first year of trading. (20)

10 John has an 'overdraft facility' of £300 from the bank in addition to his loan. During which months will he exceed it? What courses of action are open to him in this situation? (5)

11 What do you think are the main reasons for John's early cash flow problems? To what extent do you think that they were avoidable? (10)

John decided against taking on a partner but felt that he did need some help in the workshop. He advertised for an assistant and was somewhat disappointed when only two people applied. One was a young man who had not worked since school and had no qualifications in woodwork whatsoever, but who did appear to be very keen to learn. The other was a young lady who had just completed a City and Guilds Certificate in woodwork at the local technical college. John was uneasy about her, though. She appeared to have rather a strong personality that he felt might clash with his and he just did not think that a woman would be as good at the job as a man – and felt very strongly that it was 'man's work'. He gave the man the job. Not surprisingly the woman was aggrieved – she felt that this was a clear case of discrimination.

12 What grounds did she have for thinking that she had been unfairly treated? (5)

13 Name the law that she felt had been violated; quote a relevant part of it that deals with such cases as this. (5)

14 Name the commission that would deal with this case if the woman appealed to them. Compose a letter that they might send to John explaining how, in their view, he has violated the law. (10)

15 This case is perhaps not entirely straightforward. John did feel that there might be a personality clash and he *does* have to work very closely with whomever he appoints. Compose a letter that he might send in reply, defending his action. (10)

16 You are the chairperson of the commission. Compose a memorandum to the other members of the commission giving your judgement – and reasons – on the basis of the arguments that you have heard. (10)

17 If it is found that somebody has suffered from discrimination what remedies are there by way of compensation? (5)

(134)

10.3 Harris and Son Engineering Ltd

Harris and Son Engineering Ltd had enjoyed good **industrial relations** for many years. The company was an old established family firm that had been in business for nearly 100 years. It employed a workforce of 250 and many of the workers' fathers – and in some cases grandfathers – had worked for the company. Of course the generally excellent personal relations that were enjoyed between management and workers did not mean that the workers did not want a trade union to represent them. In fact there were three unions in the plant: one for the electricians, one for the engineers and one for the rest of the workers – unskilled labourers and the like. The office staff chose not to join a union. Each group of union members had a **shop steward** who was elected by the workers to negotiate with management; to 'co-ordinate' their activities they formed a **joint shop stewards committee** which, wherever possible, negotiated on important issues on behalf of the whole workforce who were in a union.

1 Explain, in your own words, the meaning of the words in **bold.** (3)
2 Why had there generally been good relations between workers and management? (6)
3 Which trade unions would be likely to represent the three groups of workers? In each case, is the union: (a) craft; (b) industrial; (c) white collar; (d) general? (6)
4 Why did the unions think that it was better if the joint shop stewards committee negotiated with management? Why might it sometimes not be possible? (8)

On the management side considerable effort was made to maintain relations with the workforce. There was a personnel officer in charge of industrial relations and he had three assistants, one of whom was responsible for staff welfare – checking that working conditions were safe and comfortable, running a sickness benefit scheme, supervising the canteen which offered cheap lunches and free coffee and overseeing the company sports and social club which had just opened a new building that included a bar, snooker tables and a squash court. He always organised at least one staff outing per year.

5 Explain why the firm may have made such efforts on staff welfare. You may wish to refer to 'Maslow's Hierarchy of Needs' (Unit 4, Section 4.2) to help your explanation. (10)

Another aspect of policy that had helped maintain good relations was the firm's tradition of offering their workers a pay increase each year that was nearly always higher than the rate of inflation, i.e. rising prices. This meant that the workers always felt that their standard of living was rising – a very welcome feeling.

6 Why does a pay increase higher than the rate of inflation lead to rising living standards? (10)

This year things were not looking so good, however. The British engineering industry was facing increased competition from abroad, particularly from countries in the European Community. Harris's order books were far emptier than could be remembered. The problem had been worsened by some complaints from customers about late delivery and the sub-standard quality of some of the items. The Managing Director called in representatives of the joint shop stewards committee for a meeting.

'I have to be honest with you, ladies and gentlemen. I am worried. You have seen the figures for orders and I think that you understand the various reasons why we are in this position. If we grant the usual wage increase our profit margin practically disappears and, apart from anything else, that would not be good news for jobs next year. As it is, we must lose fifteen members of staff. I would hope to avoid compulsory redundancies, but that would need your co-operation on a number of other fronts.'

7 What are the 'various reasons' why the firm is in a bad position? Explain why countries in the EC might cause particular problems. (8)

8 Why is a reduced profit margin not good news for jobs? (5)

9 Explain the various ways in which compulsory redundancies might be avoided. Why will this need the unions' 'co-operation'? (6)

The union representatives were horrified. They had *always* enjoyed a pay increase and there had *never* been talk of redundancies. Their first response was to talk about 'industrial action', but it seemed to some of them that this might make the problem worse. Nevertheless there was a short strike – the first in the history of the company. It was obvious that this would lose even more orders, however, and the workers soon returned. They did maintain some more limited forms of industrial action, however, while the joint shop stewards' committee negotiated with the management. In the end a 'rescue plan' was agreed which did avoid compulsory redundancies but which ensured greatly reduced job opportunities within the firm, and harder work for those working there. As part of the 'fight against inflation' as well as for the 'sake of the company' the unions agreed to waive their pay increase for the year.

10 This 'rescue plan' may well not be popular with the workers. Using your answer to question 9 and also the clues in the final paragraph, write a speech that might be delivered by one of the shop stewards explaining exactly what measures had been agreed and why they were necessary. (15)

(77)

10.4 The Hat Game

The Hat Game is a practical exercise in production management. The number of workers can be organised between you in groups, each with a game leader, depending on the numbers available. The different jobs are:

- Production Manager
- Supervisor
- Production workers
- Quality control
- Observers
- Game leader

The Production Manager

You are the manager of a hat factory. You have *ten minutes* to plan and organise your factory before production starts.

Your job is to organise a factory to make and sell paper hats. You are directly responsible to the Managing Director for the success of the factory.

You must make sure that work is provided for your work-force in each of the following areas:

(a) the tasks on the production line;
(b) supervision of the production line;
(c) quality control;
(d) raw materials;
(e) sales;
(f) wages.

(Raw materials – paper, equipment, etc. – are available for sale from the game leaders. The game leaders will also buy your hats.)

- **Production**
  You *must* produce at least 20 hats per working day.
- **Quality**
  Hats must be clean, correctly shaped, neatly folded.
- **Times**
  A working day is 10 minutes, with a rest of 1 minute at the end of each session.
- **Wages**
  Manager: Five Smarties per 10-minute day
  Supervisor: Three Smarties per day
  Quality control: Two Smarties per day
  Workers: One Smartie per day
  Wages are paid to each worker at the end of every 10-minute session.
- **Purchasing sales and finance**
  Paper is available from the game leaders at *ten* sheets per Smartie.
  The game leaders will buy hats at a price of *one* Smartie per hat, but unfortunately are only able to accept products in packs of five.
  Loans are available at a daily rate of 20 per cent.

- **Communication**
  Once the factory starts you, as the manager, must not deal directly with the work-force; your supervisors, etc. should do this for you.

The product

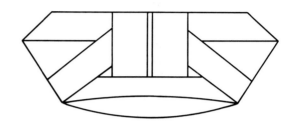

Fig. 10.2   The turban complete

Supervisor

Your job is to organise the work directly on the production line.

Once jobs have been given any changes must be agreed by you. Workers should not be asked to do a job they have not been trained for. It is a factory rule that workers stay in their work-place during work time. A working day is **10 minutes** with **1 minute** rest at the end of each session. Wages are paid at the end of each day (10 minutes).

- **Quality**
  Hats must be produced which are well folded and clean. You are responsible for maintaining quality on the line. If quality control returns a hat you must stop production while a replacement is made.
- **Payment**
  You will receive three Smarties per working day.

Quality control

Each hat must be:

(a) neatly folded;
(b) clean;
(c) of the correct shape.

If you detect a hat of poor quality, you must return it to the supervisor. Wages are paid at the end of each working day (10 minutes).

- **Payment**
  You earn two Smarties per day.

Production line

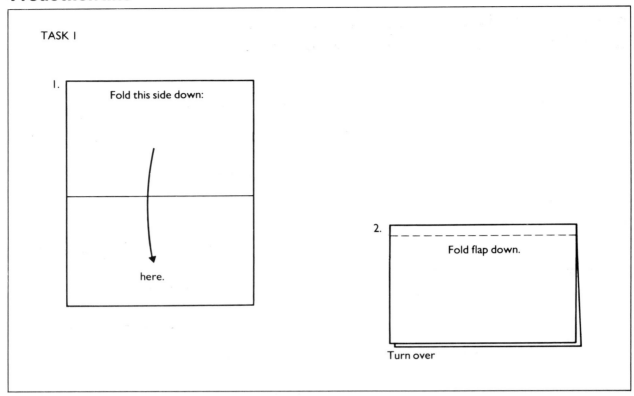

TASK 1

1. Fold this side down: here.

2. Fold flap down.
Turn over

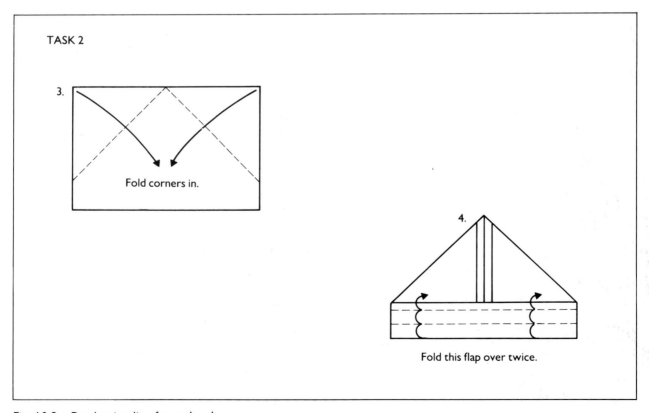

TASK 2

3. Fold corners in.

4. Fold this flap over twice.

Fig. 10.3   Production line for turban hat

TASK 3

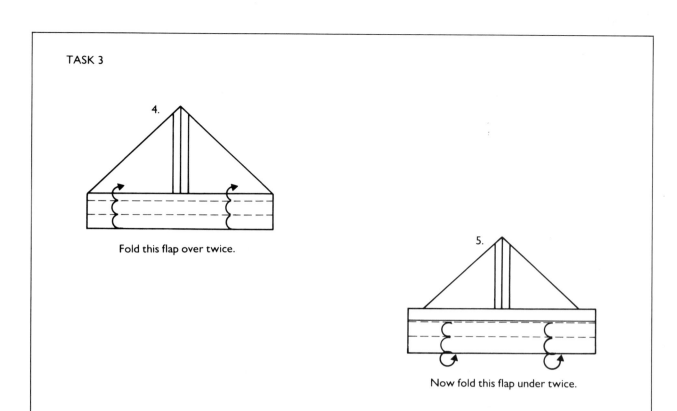

4.

Fold this flap over twice.

5.

Now fold this flap under twice.

TASK 4

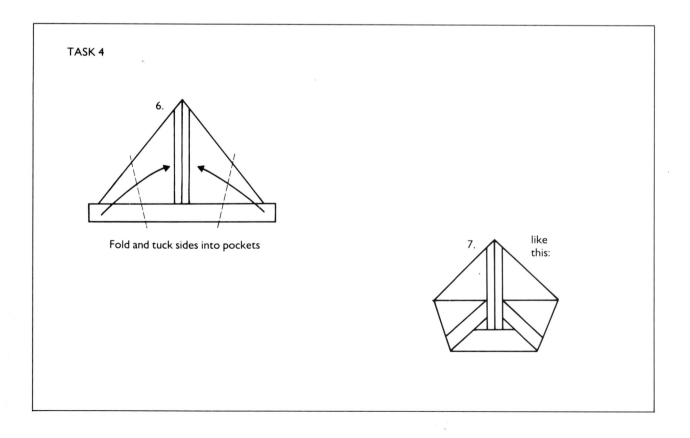

6.

Fold and tuck sides into pockets

7.

like this:

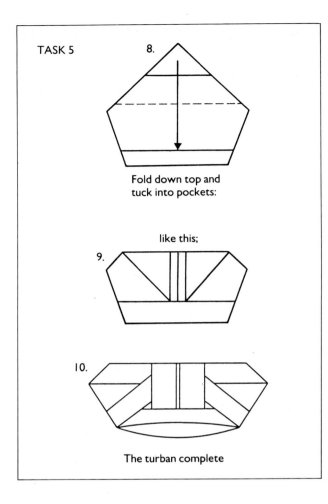

TASK 5

8.

Fold down top and
tuck into pockets:

like this;

9.

10.

The turban complete

Production workers

1 If you do not understand your task, ask your supervisor.
2 You will be paid one Smartie for every **10 minutes'** work.
3 During work time you *must* stay in your work-place.
4 Any change in the work you do must be agreed with your supervisor.
5 You are not allowed to do anyone else's job.

Observers

Your job is to watch what each member of the team does, and to assess their skills and attitudes in the following ways:

- communication;
- responsibility;
- coping;
- communication;
- team spirit.

1 Was each individual involved and to what extent?
2 How did the leader find out and use the particular talents of each member of the team?
3 How did the leader encourage the individuals?
4 How did the members of the team cope with problems?
5 Did the team 'talk' to the supervisor?
6 Did the team show responsibility for:
   (a) each other;
   (b) the product;
   (c) the company?

10.5 The Tyne and Wear Metro

Cost - benefit analysis

Cost-benefit analysis helps to decide whether a project is worth while or not. It is usually applied to projects in the public sector – in other words to those introduced by the government or a local authority.

Very briefly, it judges the project by comparing the social benefits – the 'good things' for the community – with the social costs – the 'bad things' for the community (see Unit 1, Section 1.5). The project is worth while if the benefits are greater than the costs.

The following case study, based on the development of the Metro in the Newcastle-upon-Tyne area, helps to show how the method works.

What is the Tyne and Wear Metro?

(Press release – January 1983)
'The Metro is a system of light rapid transit running on segregated track mainly over the route of the old London and North-Eastern Railway Tyneside electric train services which were de-electrified and converted to diesel multiple-unit operation by British Railways in the 1960s. Some of the track is newly built, some single and some double track. It is electrified at 1,500 volts direct current (d.c.) with overhead conductors.

Stations are unmanned with ticket-operated turnstiles. Tickets are obtained from automatic machines which give change. As trains arrive at stations automatic displays indicate destinations. Public address announcements can be made at stations from the Central Control Centre at South Gosforth.

There are now over 30 miles of Metro route serving north and south Tyneside. The Queen Elizabeth Bridge of Heworth carries the Metro over the Tyne on the longest of the river's six bridges (538 feet span). North and south of the bridge the line goes underground below the cities of Newcastle and Gateshead.

Overall the system represents a major new initiative in urban transport provision. Passenger use in 1982 was nearly 20 per cent higher than forecast. Users have certainly taken to the system very well, although there have been some complaints about noise. The Passenger Transport Executive, responsible for the design and operation of the Metro, is considering further track modification to reduce the noise problem and is also considering further line extensions.'

Examine the map (Fig. 10.4) carefully to identify the route of the present Metro and the areas it serves.

The plan to develop a new rail system in Newcastle, Gateshead and along the River Tyne to the coast at Tynemouth, Whitley Bay and South Shields was first published in 1971. There was growing traffic congestion in inner cities and a strong feeling that the public should be encouraged to use public transport again.

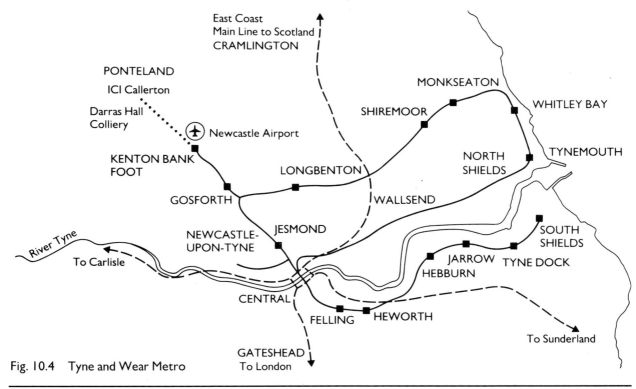

Fig. 10.4   Tyne and Wear Metro

Back to public transport

If it is believed that the public *should* go back to public transport there are really five possible systems:

1 bus lanes (and 'contraflow' lanes) to make journeys by bus in and out of cities much quicker;
2 better and more frequent bus and train services;
3 cheaper (subsidised) fares and/or cut-price tickets for regular users (season tickets);
4 much higher car-park charges;
5 road closures, parking restrictions, one-way schemes, etc., to discourage private car drivers.

The first three of these are known as 'carrot' solutions – to encourage public transport users – while the latter are 'stick' methods – to discourage private cars.

The Tyne and Wear Metro system was designed along the lines of 'better and more frequent bus and train services' – but with a revolutionary and imaginative strategy.

The Metro scheme

The scheme was first opened in November 1982. The system has a total length of 34 miles, using British Rail track along with a new underground system and some elevated track (along Japanese principles of mass transport).

Small local stations were re-opened and some new stations were built. Metro trains are two-car units. They are one-man operated and drivers have a radio link with a control centre. Stations are mainly unstaffed, access to platforms is by ticket-operated barriers and passengers can obtain tickets and change from automatic machines.

Fares are on a zone basis and are integrated with a bus network so that bus/metro tickets are available. Travelcards offer a discount to regular travellers. Fares are at economic rates, which means that they are not particularly cheap as in Sheffield or London, but the service is quick, modern, clean and efficient, making Metro travel attractive to a lot of people who would otherwise use private cars.

The new stations serve growing housing areas where, in many cases, buses from a number of localities link with the Metro (Fig. 10.5) and where they can often pull up right outside the station entrance.

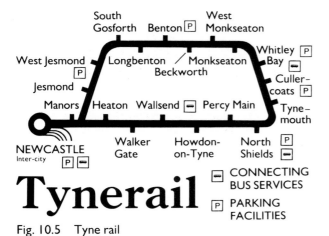

Fig. 10.5 Tyne rail

Further extensions

The first Metro sections were opened in 1978 and the main costs of the total scheme were absorbed by the eight miles of new underground track and the interchanges. The new steel bridge across the Tyne between Central Station and Gateshead was also a major cost. The rest of the surface track simply used existing local British Rail lines. The latest elevated sections are now in use and attention is focused on further extensions. One such link might join Kenton Bank Foot to the airport.

The industrial structures of Tyne and Wear

It is generally agreed that the future prosperity of the north-east region lies in a major change in its industrial structure. Traditional industries – steel-making, coal-mining, ship-building and chemical manufacture – are in serious decline. New industries have been difficult to encourage into the region. Micro-technology, light assembly, etc. have tended to develop in the south. Regional unemployment averages over 18 per cent and there are pockets in excess of 25–30 per cent. Youth unemployment, in particular, is a major problem.

One important measure to encourage new firms to develop in the north-east is the improvement in the 'infrastructure'. This means government and local investment in local services, in particular better housing, road improvements, including motorways, factories to let and airport development. This latter facility is very important because the Newcastle area is so remote from the financial and business centres of the south. If major multinational companies are to be encouraged to set up factories and offices in or around Newcastle, good communications are important.

Metro extension to Newcastle Airport

Beyond the terminus of the Metro at Kenton Bank Foot is an existing mineral railway line to Darras Hall Colliery and its nearby ICI chemical works. This passes close to the airport terminus buildings and it seems natural that Metro services should be extended to a new station at the airport (see Fig. 10.6). This line would still prove expensive to construct but should confer important advantages for airport users and, therefore, for those interested in the economic development of the region.

Some people would be inconvenienced by a further Metro service near their homes and the decision to develop the line here could mean a lack of service to a community elsewhere. However, firms considering coming to the region would offer new employment opportunities. An airport linked to the local transport network could prove a major factor for some multinationals. Paying for the line would depend on ticket sales but there would also be hidden gains to local administrations through lower traffic congestion on roads to and from the airport. It would be difficult to judge how important such a rail link might be in the successful further development of the airport, but all factors have to be considered in the final decision over any local infrastructure improvement – housing estate, hospital, bypass, shopping centre or whatever.

Social and private costs

If the Metro link were to be privately financed only private costs and benefits would be considered; financial receipts from ticket sales would be set against construction costs, running costs, land purchase, etc. Since the decision to extend the system lies in the hands of national and local authorities, social costs and benefits can be included – indirect benefits from improved airport access, shorter journey times, less local traffic congestion, etc.

A final decision on the viability of an airport Metro link would depend on all these factors – costs on one hand set against the benefits on the other.

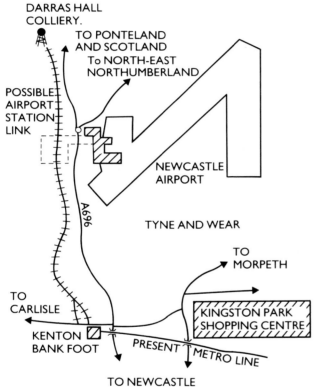

Fig. 10.6   Newcastle Airport/Colliery link

EXERCISE

1   You are required to produce a 200-word article for a national newspaper under the heading 'North-east Transport Revolution'. Read through the press release at the beginning of the case study and prepare your article. Try to keep to the 200 word limit.

2   Consider carefully the alternative systems suggested earlier in this case study for solving the problem of urban passenger transport. Compare the advantages of the 'carrot' and 'stick' solutions – you might like to draw up a table to summarise your views.

3   Explain what is meant by the following terms:
   (a)   economic rates (or fares);
   (b)   an integrated road and rail system;
   (c)   multinational companies;
   (d)   infrastructure.

4   A **logo** is used to advertise the service and keep it in the public mind. Think of rail logos like the British Rail 'arrows' and the London Underground circle and bar. Design a Metro logo, bearing in mind the need to be modern, original and eye-catching.

EXTENSION ACTIVITY

1   **Social costs and benefits**
   (a)   What are the *social benefits* which would be gained from an improved communication link between central Newcastle and its airport via the Metro extension from Kenton Bank Foot? In your answer, consider factors such as reduced road congestion; improved travel times for air travellers; safety aspects; attraction for industry; other issues you think are important.
   (b)   On the other hand, there are *social costs* involved in the scheme: for example, inconvenience to residents from increased airport use; a new Metro line; loss of land to farmers and others; possible burden on ratepayers.
      Write a brief report summarising the two sides of the argument and conclude with your own view.

2   **Financial costs and benefits**
   (a)   What are the *financial costs* which are likely to be involved in a Metro extension? Consider factors such as costs of new track, signalling, etc.; new stations and facilities – including car park extension at Kenton Bank Foot; development of the new airport concourse; running and maintenance costs – including depreciation.
   (b)   What *financial benefits* would be gained by operating the service? Consider, for example, ticket sales; catering revenue; advertising revenue.
      Produce a table to summarise the two sides of the argument.

GROUP ACTIVITY

Stage a public enquiry into the proposed Metro extension: Kenton Bank Foot to Newcastle Airport. You will need the appropriate Department of the Environment officials, a Chairperson, etc. and a series of representatives of interested groups such as the following:

(a) a local government group;
(b) Newcastle Taxi Operators Committee;
(c) Northumberland County Council (landowners);
(d) a local farmer (landowners);
(e) Secretary of the local Residents' Association;
(f) Newcastle Ratepayers' representative;
(g) National Union of Railwaymen;
(h) Chairperson of the Passenger Transport Executive (who run the Metro);
(i) Metro solicitor.

The enquiry and the speeches made can be recorded and examined in a de-briefing session.

FOR DISCUSSION

The north-east is a relatively remote region from the more prosperous areas of southern England. It needs motorways and a fast rail service to give improved links with the south. It also needs a successful airport.

Why is airport development important to industrial prosperity in remote areas of the EC? What does this indicate about the future of industry in the regions of Britain? What are the advantages and disadvantages of air over rail travel in this case?

Hold a class discussion to work out the importance of air links and their advantages and disadvantages to businesses throughout EC countries.

Index

Index compiled by Peva Keane